Ramya Nagesh is a barrister at 4-5 Gray's Inn Square. She has spent over fifteen years in the law, with well over eleven of those at the Bar. After almost a decade building a successful criminal practice, she chose to focus primarily on another area in which she was being instructed more and more: inquests.

Ramya has acted in the widest range of inquests: from those lasting less than a day where she is the only advocate, up to those of the greatest public interest. Some of the most recent inquests in which she has acted include an inquest into the death of a man beheaded by a person suffering from severe mental difficulties, an inquest into the sudden death of a man whilst he was being arrested and the Inquest into the Terror Attacks at the Fishmonger's Hall in November 2019.

A Practical Guide to the Law in Relation to Inquests

A Practical Guide to the Law in Relation to Inquests

Ramya Nagesh

Barrister (Lincoln's Inn)

LLB (Hons), MSc (LSE)

Law Brief Publishing

Published 2023 by Law Brief Publishing, an imprint of Law Brief Publishing Ltd
30 The Parks
Minehead
Somerset
TA24 8BT

www.lawbriefpublishing.com

Paperback: 978-1-916698-06-2

For Malini

PREFACE

Since at least 1194 and the 'Articles of Eyre' we have had a coronial system. Back then, the principle aims were not anything nearly as worthy as seeking justice or finding the truth. The coroner was primarily tasked to 'keep the pleas of the Crown', with the investigation of death being a convenient second task. In a feudal world where the Crown's purse could be directly impacted by the death of one of its subjects, we can see why the proper investigation of any unnatural or suspicious death (with fines available to the coroner for any community which failed to explain a death to his satisfaction) was of importance to the Crown.

As the centuries have rolled by, the coronial system has thankfully evolved. It is now an entrenched part of a legal system that strives to keep justice and transparency at its core. Many of us within the legal profession are building more and more inquest work into our practices, or even taking the plunge and sitting as coroners. It is easy to understand why: in a coronial case, the legal professional can have the chance to analyse and argue about complex legal issues, exercise their skills of witness-handling and be a key part of some of the most important public interest cases in modern times. More than that, though, at the heart of every single inquest is a person who has died in circumstances which are violent, unnatural or unexplained. That means there is often also a devastated family who just want to know the truth about what happened to their loved one – a sobering reminder of how important these cases are in which we practice.

So we may know why we are interested in inquest work, but taking on those first few cases can feel daunting. An inquest hearing does not look like the civil or criminal courtrooms which many practitioners may be used to. In an inquest it is the coroner – rather than the advocates – who chooses which witnesses are to be called, leads questioning of those witnesses and decides which evidence is relevant to the issues at hand.

Nevertheless, advocates must work incredibly hard to ensure that their client's interests are protected and their aims furthered.

This book is intended to assist all those within the profession and beyond to grasp the fundamental elements of a coronial investigation and inquest from beginning to end. It is designed to give you all the practical and theoretical knowledge you will need without being overwhelming – the sort of book that you can toss into your bag for court and rely upon.

The law is ever-changing, and that is particularly true for the law in relation to inquests. Therefore, it is incumbent upon me to make clear that the law in this book is up to date as of the date of writing: 5 October 2023.

Ramya Nagesh
October 2023

CONTENTS

PART ONE

THE BUILDING BLOCKS OF AN INQUEST

CHAPTER ONE

THE BACKGROUND TO AN INQUEST

SOURCES OF LAW AND PROCEDURE

CORONERS AND JUSTICE ACT 2009

The morning of 25 July 2013 heralded the coming into force of a ground-breaking piece of legislation in the history of inquest law: the Coroners and Justice Act 2009 ("the 2009 Act"). It is that statute which continues to govern inquest law today, some ten years later. Its predecessor was the Coroners Act 1988 which, despite the similarity in name, was in fact a consolidating Act pulling together statutes from the 19th Century, rather than the coherent piece of legislation which the 2009 Act promised to be. Before the 1988 Act was the 1887 Act, which itself was a consolidation of a number of ancient statutes passed mainly in the reigns of Edward I, Edward III and Henry VIII.

The 2009 Act was long overdue in the opinion of many: there had been decades of discontent which would bubble over into loud calls for reform of the coronial system. For example:

- The killing of anti-racist campaigner Blair Peach in 1979 was alleged by witnesses to have been caused by a police officer. At least one pathologist concluded that the injury to Peach's skull could have been caused by a lead-weighted cosh or police radio. An internal police investigation concluded that Peach was almost certainly killed by a police officer. That report was never disclosed to the inquest into Peach's death; it was only released 31 years later. As a result, at least partially, the inquest that had taken place found the death was caused by 'misadventure';

- The report of the Stephen Lawrence Inquiry – a landmark report in many ways – was published in 1999 and made recommendations in relation to the way in which inquests were conducted. The report reflected the inquiry's view that the overall inquest system was no longer fit for purpose. It made recommendations such as advance disclosure of evidence to parties who had leave to appear at the inquest, and legal aid to be provided to the bereaved families;

- Medical-related scandals led to calls for reform of the coronial system, culminating in the conviction of Dr Harold Shipman for the murder of 15 of his patients;

- A major review led by Tom Luce into the coronial system led to a hefty 300-plus-page report being published in 2003. That report said that inquests must undergo "*radical change if they are to become fit for the purposes of a modern society*"[1]. That report drew attention to numerous deficiencies with the system at the time, including lack of sustained training of coroners, lack of legal and medical expertise, lack of resources and processes for working with other public bodies and the basis for coronial law being archaic, ancient structures.

As a result of events such as these, the Coroners Bill 2006 was created; it eventually find statutory footing as the Coroners and Justice Act 2009.

The 2009 Act made a number of changes to coronial law, which included:

[1] *Death Certification and investigation in England, Wales and Northern Ireland. The report of a Fundamental Review 2003*, chaired by Tom Luce, at paragraph 3; available at https://webarchive.nationalarchives.gov.uk/ukgwa/20131205105739/http://www.archive2.official-documents.co.uk/document/cm58/5831/5831.pdf, last accessed on 5 October 2023

- The introduction of the concept of an 'investigation' led by a coroner, of which the inquest represented the final part. This meant that inquests need not be opened every time a death was referred to the coroner and so lead to a reduced number of inquests;

- The appointment for the first time of a Chief Coroner;

- Changes to the circumstances in which a coroner must summon a jury;

- Appointments of Medical Examiners (*this is only in force from 1 October 2023*);

- Abolishing the office of Coroner of the Queen's Household. Now any investigation or inquest passes to the coroner area in which the body is found.

The 2009 Act is the backbone to the inquest work which you, as coroners, practitioners, or interested persons, will be undertaking.

The 2009 Act does not solely relate to inquests. However, this is a book about inquests and so we shall focus only on those provisions which do govern inquests. Those sections have, by and large, been in force since 25 July 2013. There are various amendments which will come into force from 2024. If those amendments are relevant to a particular issue discussed in this book, they will be highlighted at the appropriate point.

The 2009 Act applies to all inquests which have taken place after 25 July 2013, regardless of when the death occurred. So for example, the most recent inquest into the deaths that occurred as a result of the Hillsborough Stadium tragedy in 1989 was governed by the 2009 Act, notwithstanding that the deaths the inquest investigated took place long before the Act's commencement.

CORONERS (INVESTIGATIONS) REGULATIONS 2013

Section 43 of the 2009 Act provides the Lord Chancellor with the power to make regulations "*at or in connection with investigations … (other than the practice and procedure at or in connection with inquests*[2]". As a result, we have the Coroners (Investigations) Regulations 2013 ("the 2013 Investigation Regulations").

The explanatory notes to the 2013 Investigation Regulations tell us that:

> "*These Regulations regulate the practice and procedure relating to investigations into deaths carried out under Part 1 of the Coroners and Justice Act 2009 ("the 2009 Act").*
>
> *Part 1 of the 2009 Act introduced a new regime for death investigations, which replaces the Coroners Act 1988 and the Coroners Rules 1984. Under the 2009 Act a coroner must conduct an investigation into violent or unnatural deaths, deaths where the cause is unknown and deaths which occur in custody or otherwise in state detention. In certain cases this investigation will include the coroner holding an inquest.*
>
> *These Regulations form part of a package of new rules and regulations made under the 2009 Act which come into force at the same time as these Regulations.*[3]"

The Regulations make provision for matters relating to the investigation as a whole, such as the keeping of a register of reported deaths, providing information to the next of kin or personal representative of the deceased, the timing and arrangements in relation to post-mortem examination and transfer of investigations and the release of bodies for burial.

---

[2] Section 43(1)(a) of the 2009 Act

[3] Para 1 of Explanatory Note to the 2013 Investigation Regulations

We will therefore find that, as this book focuses on the inquest process, we naturally do not refer to the 2013 Investigation Regulations as we may perhaps do with other sources of law and guidance.

Regulation 26 is of importance to the inquest process, when we consider in later chapters the duty of the coroner to complete an inquest within a specific expedient period of time. By virtue of Regulation 26, the coroner must notify the Chief Coroner of any investigation which has not been completed or discontinued within a year of that death being reported. The coroner must also provide explanation as to why this is the case.

Additionally, Part 7 of the 2013 Investigations Regulations is of importance to those of us focusing on the inquest process. Part 7 deals with action to prevent further deaths. This ties in with paragraph 7 of schedule 5 to the 2009 Act, which provides that the coroner has a duty to make a report for the prevention of deaths in similar circumstances when certain criteria are met. We will deal with this in further detail in Chapter 14.

CORONERS (INQUESTS) RULES 2013

The Coroners (Inquests) Rules 2013 ("the 2013 Inquests Rules") came into force on the same day as the 2009 Act and replaced the Coroners Rules 1984. These Rules provide a set of procedural standards for the conduct of inquests and pre-inquest reviews.

The 2013 Inquests Rules make provision for matters such as the disclosure of documents, the management of the inquest hearing, admissibility of evidence, the summoning of juries and the record of the findings of the inquest.

One significant new development in the 2013 Inquests Rules was the provision of a statutory basis for pre-inquest review hearings. Before the 2013 Inquests Rules, pre-inquest reviews had taken place but they had not had any basis in the legislation: they had been conducted informally by coroners who recognised the need for greater case management in some of their cases.

CHIEF CORONER'S GUIDANCE AND LAW SHEETS

Since the appointment of the first Chief Coroner through the 2009 Act, those of us practising in coronial law have had the benefit of a number of guidance documents and law sheets produced by the Chief Coroner.

They are all to be found online, on the Courts and Tribunals Judiciary website[4], and provide an invaluable set of resources for practitioners and coroners alike.

The guidance documents (of which there are currently 41) cover subjects ranging from the location of inquests and the appointment of coroners to the conduct of pre-inquest reviews, the conduct of inquests held entirely in writing and the framing of conclusions. They tend to be a few pages in length each and provide comprehensive but succinct guidance around their specific issues. Where there is guidance that is relevant to the particular subject that we are considering in this book, I include reference to that guidance at the appropriate points.

The law sheets (of which there are currently five) take similar form to the guidance documents but are focused on specific areas of law rather than practice or policy. For example, there is a lawsheet covering the topic of hearsay evidence, and a lawsheet covering the conclusion of unlawful killing. Again, where a law sheet exists which is relevant to the particular subject that we are considering in this book, I include reference to that sheet at the appropriate point.

Coroners do not act under the authority of the Chief Coroner, and they have their own independence in relation to their own inquest, so do not technically need to follow either the guidance or the law sheets. However, it is clear to see that an application to judicially review the decision of a coroner who has failed to follow the guidance of the Chief Coroner may

[4] https://www.judiciary.uk/courts-and-tribunals/coroners-courts/coroners-legislation-guidance-and-advice/coroners-guidance/, last accessed 5 October 2023.

have more weight than one which seeks to review the actions of a coroner who has paid heed to these documents.

KEY PEOPLE

There are a number of key people who feature in inquest proceedings. In brief, they are as follows.

THE CORONER

Each inquest will have, at its head, the coroner. They will not only be steering the course of the inquest but will be making all major legal and procedural decisions – determining what evidence to call, questioning witnesses and ultimately reaching conclusions.

Within the inquest system as a whole, though, there are different types of coroners.

The Chief Coroner

At the head of the coronial system sits the Chief Coroner, whose appointment we have touched upon. The post of Chief Coroner was first created by Schedule 8 to the 2009 Act. The Chief Coroner is the national head of the coronial system.

The Lord Chief Justice appoints the Chief Coroner (paragraph 1(1) of Schedule 8 to the 2009 Act). The Lord Chief Justice must consult the Lord Chancellor about both the appointment and the duration of the term of office.

The appointee must be a High Court Judge or a Circuit Judge who is under the age of 70. On the date of writing (5 October 2023) the Chief Coroner is Thomas Teague KC.

The Chief Coroner has a number of powers and duties:

- To conduct inquests;

- To receive reports of all inquests and to make an annual report to the Lord Chief Justice;
- To control and take over the issue of reports on action to prevent future deaths;
- To have responsibility for the training of coroners;
- To maintain links with the Ministry of Justice Coroners Reform Team, the Judicial College and the Office of Judicial Complaints;
- To issue guidance dealing with issues that might arise in practice;
- To approve future coroner appointments;
- To keep a register of coroner investigations lasting more than twelve months, and to take steps to reduce unnecessary delays;
- To monitor investigations into deaths of service personnel overseas;
- To oversee transfers of cases between coroners;
- To provide an annual report on the coroner system to the Lord Chancellor, which is to be laid before Parliament;
- To collate, monitor and publish coroners' reports to prevent future deaths;
- To direct coroners to conduct investigations in specific circumstances.

Deputy Chief Coroners

The Lord Chief Justice may appoint as many Deputy Chief Coroners as they consider appropriate. At the time of writing (5 October 2023) there are two Deputy Chief Coroners in post. The Lord Chief Justice must consult the Lord Chancellor about the appropriate numbers of Deputy Chief Coroners, and about the question of many should be judges and how many should be senior coroners / coroner for treasure.

The appointee must be a High Court Judge, a Circuit Judge, the coroner for treasure or a senior coroner. They must also be under 70 years of age. The term of office is determined between the Lord Chief Justice and the Lord Chancellor.

Senior Coroners, Assistant Coroners and Area Coroners

Before the 2009 Act, coroner areas were known as 'coroner districts'. The 2009 Act amended the positions of coroners under the old coroner districts and added a new position of area coroner.

- Senior coroners under the 2009 Act are the same as coroners under the Coroners Act 1988. There is one senior coroner per area;

- Assistant coroners under the 2009 Act are the same as deputy coroners / assistant deputy coroners under the Coroners Act 1988. Each area should have a minimum of one assistant coroner;

- Area coroners are an entirely new post. They are qualified in the same way as assistant coroners.

These coroners are appointed by local authorities with the agreement of the Lord Chief Justice and the Chief Coroner.

Specialist Coroners

The Chief Coroner has created a specialist cadre of coroners in England and Wales. These are coroners who are specially trained and conduct investigations and inquests into service and military deaths. They deal with deaths overseas and those that take place in England and Wales.

INTERESTED PERSONS

Unlike civil or criminal proceedings, which may be the usual stomping ground of many practitioners who are new to inquests, an inquest is not a strict adversarial process. It follows that there are no 'parties' to the inquest, as there are no 'sides'.

However, there are 'interested persons' – they are people recognised by the court as having a particular interest in the proceedings. The concept of 'interested persons' in the 2009 Act replaces the old concept of 'properly interested persons' that was previously in place under the Coroners Rules 1984. Other than the change in name, there seems to be little significant difference between them.

Who can be an interested person?

The coroner leading the inquest designates which people or organisations can be given 'interested person' status, by reference to the statute.

Section 47 of the 2009 Act sets out the categories of people who are to be considered 'interested persons':

> "*47* ***"Interested person"***
>
> *(1) This section applies for the purposes of this Part.*
>
> *(2) "Interested person" , in relation to a deceased person or an investigation or inquest under this Part into a person's death, means—*
>
>> *(a) a spouse, civil partner, partner, parent, child, brother, sister, grandparent, grandchild, child of a brother or sister, stepfather, stepmother, half-brother or half-sister;*
>>
>> *(b) a personal representative of the deceased;*
>>
>> *(c) a medical examiner exercising functions in relation to the death of the deceased;*

(d) a beneficiary under a policy of insurance issued on the life of the deceased;

(e) the insurer who issued such a policy of insurance;

(f) a person who may by any act or omission have caused or contributed to the death of the deceased, or whose employee or agent may have done so;

(g) in a case where the death may have been caused by—

(i) an injury received in the course of an employment, or

(ii) a disease prescribed under section 108 of the Social Security Contributions and Benefits Act 1992 (c. 4) (benefit in respect of prescribed industrial diseases, etc),

a representative of a trade union of which the deceased was a member at the time of death;

(h) a person appointed by, or representative of, an enforcing authority;

(i) where subsection (3) applies, a chief constable;

(j) where subsection (4) applies, a Provost Marshal [of a service police force or of the tri-service serious crime unit]1 ;

(k) where subsection (5) applies, the [Director General of the Independent Office for Police Conduct]2 ;

(ka) where subsection (5A) applies, the Service Police Complaints Commissioner;

(l) a person appointed by a Government department to attend [or follow]4 an inquest into the death or to assist in, or provide evidence for the purposes of, an investigation into the death under this Part;

> *(m) any other person who the senior coroner thinks has a sufficient interest.*"

It is worth noting that, despite the long list of relatively specific categories, the coroner retains discretion to appoint as an interested person anyone who does not otherwise fit into the section 47 of the 2009 Act. This is provided for by the 'sweep-up' provision in section 47(2)(m) of the 2009 Act.

What rights does an interested person have?

Where a person is designated as an interested person their rights include:

- To be notified of the date, time and place of the inquest hearing (Coroners (Inquests) Rules 2013, r.9(2)) and to attend the same;

- Subject to any restrictions on disclosure arising under r.15 of the Coroners (Inquests) Rules 2013, to be provided with a document or a copy of that document (Coroners (Inquests) Rules 2013, r.13(1));

- To examine any witness either in person or through their representative (Coroners (Inquests) Rules 2013, r.19(1)); and

- To make submissions to the coroner on matters such as conclusions.

Relevant cases

R v Greater London (South District) Coroner ex parte Driscoll (1995) 159 JP 45:

The sister of the deceased sought to judicially review the coroner's decision that she was not a properly interested person under the Coroners Rules 1984. In allowing the application, the Court held that close blood relations who were in contact with the deceased before he died are interested persons for the purposes of the Rules. The coroner had been wrong to take into account the acrimonious relationship between the applicant and the deceased's wife.

Some key points from the case are:

- The word 'interested' should not be given a narrow or technical meaning: it is not confined to a proprietary right or financial interest in the estate of the deceased;
- An applicant for interested person status must show that they have "*more than idle curiosity. The mere fact of being a witness will rarely be enough. What must be shown is that the person has a genuine desire to participate more than by the mere giving of relevant evidence in the determination of how, when and where the deceased came by his death.*" (*per* Kennedy LJ);
- The other categories of person in the statutory sub-paragraphs are to be used as a guide to the type of person that may qualify under the 'sweep-up' category;
- When deciding whether to grant the status of interested person, a coroner is not entitled to take into account any (no matter how understandable) desire to avoid unpleasantness or ill-feeling at the inquest. For example, it is irrelevant that members of the deceased's family may not wish a particular person to be recognised as an interested person;
- It is not helpful to look to the law on standing in Judicial Review proceedings as analogous to interested person status;
- Family relations and non-consanguineous relationships not mentioned explicitly in the legislation can be recognised as interested persons under the 'sweep-up' category.

Coroner's inquests into the London bombings of 7 July 2005 – Decision following pre-inquest hearing from 26 to 30 April 2010

The inquests into the deaths of 52 people killed in terrorist attacks in London was conducted by Hallet LJ. Over the course of the proceedings, she delivered various rulings which have been of assistance to practitioners and coroners since.

At the pre-inquest hearing from 26 to 30 April 2010, Hallet LJ considered various individual applications for interested person status (at that time, 'properly interested person'). Out of her decisions, it seems the following were important factors in determining that a certain person or category of persons should be interested persons (see paragraphs 122 to 136):

- Played a significant role in the events;
- A genuine desire to participate and assist the process;
- Able to offer specialist help to the investigation.

In that decision, the coroner found that the survivors did not meet the criteria for being properly interested persons. At paragraph 135 to 136:

> "*135. However, I need not dwell upon my concerns and I return to the question in hand: should I exercise my discretion in favour of designating the survivors under rule 20? I needed no reminding of the extent of the suffering of those who survived the bombs. The Scene Reports make graphic and extraordinarily distressing reading even for those of us used to horrific criminal acts. I needed no persuading that many survivors will have a valuable role to play in the resumed inquests. However, at times I confess Mr O'Connor's submissions, with great respect to him, seemed to me to be more about providing a mechanism for the survivors to obtain legal representation than the legitimate scope of designated person status under rule 20. These are inquests under a particular statutory regime. They are not a public*

inquiry under the Inquiries Act 2005 or otherwise. I have an independent legal team available to the survivors and to others to ensure issues they may wish to pursue are brought to my attention and, if I think it appropriate, canvassed in evidence. To my mind it does not require separate representation and therefore separate public funding to ensure their interests are properly protected. I intend to make sure survivors feel they are a proper part of the process. To that end, I have already authorised the release of the Scene Reports to those survivors who have signed the confidentiality undertaking. Survivors may attend the proceedings whenever they wish. Some will be called to give evidence. I shall encourage them to use the services of the Inquest Team and to ensure that we pursue all legitimate lines of inquiry and ask all relevant questions. I will read and hear submissions from them if they wish to submit them. I will ensure the process is as open as possible. A transcript of the public proceedings will be published each day on the website thereby enabling the survivors to follow them in detail. I will ensure that all survivors are treated with care and sensitivity.

136. However, as sympathetic as I feel towards them, I must bear very much in mind the primary functions of an inquest which are to inquire into the four statutory questions about the deaths and I must bear in mind the views of some of the bereaved families. I take Mr O'Connor's point that it was not clear exactly how many bereaved families are united in opposing the application to designate the nineteen survivors as interested parties, but in my judgment, there were enough. There was clear anxiety on the part of a significant number. If Mr O'Connor or any of the survivors in person had been able to identify for me issues upon which they have a unique perspective, which could only properly be reflected by their being able to ask questions, I might have decided differently. They were not. In those circumstances, I can see no proper legal basis for designating the survivors as interested persons in addition to all the others designated. There will be numerous parties represented and asking questions at the resumed inquests and there may be unrepresented parties wishing to ask questions. I will have to control them all (within reason) if I am to keep to the strict timetable I wish to set. I want the bereaved families and the survivors to have as many answers as possible and preferably by the end of the year. Adding to the list of those entitled to ask questions I fear will not assist that process."

<u>Allman v HM Coroner for West Sussex (2012) EWHC 534 (Admin)</u>

This case related to an application for interested person status by a person who, knowing the deceased in life, had made a promise to them to ensure that the death was fully and properly investigated. In upholding the coroner's refusal to accord this person interested person status, the Court stated (at paragraph 25):

"*25. It follows that the Deputy Assistant Coroner was well within her rights to refuse Mr Allman properly interested party status since his wish for that status was essentially to fulfil his promise to the deceased that he would ensure that the circumstances of his death would be fully and properly investigated by the police and the inquest process if he met his death in what might loosely be described as suspicious circumstances. Since there was no such evidence, there was no basis for his being accorded properly interested party status. Moreover, it is clear that all the relevant evidence that Mr Allman wished to place before the jury was in fact placed before the jury since it was relevant to their consideration of the deceased's state of mind. Mr Allman's wider evidence about electromagnetic weaponry in general and its propensities to kill and of its use by security forces in covert assaults on persons those forces wish to destroy or whose political protests they wish to neutralise was not relevant for the jury in this case to consider and, in any event, was prohibited from being adduced at this inquest by virtue of Rule 36 which precludes consideration of opinions and hypothetical situations which have no evidential link to the particular death being considered.*"

Platts v HM Coroner for South Yorkshire (East District) and Chief Constable of South Yorkshire Police (2008) EWHC 2502 (Admin)

The former girlfriend of the deceased was held to be a properly interested person under the Coroners Rules 1984. One of the reasons for this was the fact that her interest was genuine and directed to a proper motive, namely questioning whether the system had let the deceased down, notwithstanding that she had not been in a relationship with the deceased when he passed away.

In addition, the Court noted that the fact that a person may wish to bring a civil claim for damages as a result of the death of the deceased neither qualifies nor disqualifies them from interested person status.

Re Northern Ireland Human Rights Commission (2002) UKHL 25

This case is authority for the proposition that a public interest organisation may be recognised as an interested person in an appropriate case, even if they have no connection with or specific knowledge of the deceased. The Court held that relevant considerations include whether the group will assist the coroner to perform the role in which he or she is engaged, such as by having expertise in a relevant legal or factual area (paragraph 32).

R (Southall Black Sisters) v HM Coroner for West Yorkshire (2002) EWHC 1914 (Admin)

This was a case where the group (Southall Black Sisters) sought to rely on the ruling in *Re Northern Ireland, supra,* to argue it should have interested person status. However, in this case the Court declined to overturn the decision of the coroner. At paragraph 53:

> "*53. … It was a matter for the coroner to form an opinion whether the claimant was a properly interested person in relation to the two inquests before him. The fact that the claimant had virtually no connection with the family of the two deceased was a relevant consideration. The fact that the claimant had no direct knowledge of*

the circumstances in which the two deceased had died was a relevant factor, although not (in isolation) a conclusive one. It seems to me that the coroner in this case formed a perfectly rational decision which is not amenable to challenge by judicial review."

R v Coroner of the Queen's Household ex p Al-Fayed (2001) 58 BMLR 205

Mr Al-Fayed sought interested person status in the inquest into the death of Diana, Princess of Wales, who had died in the same car crash which killed Mr Al-Fayed's son. In considering the claim, the Divisional Court expressed approval for the coroner's proposition that Rule 20(2)(h) of the 1984 Rules (the equivalent provision to section 47(2)(m) in CAJA 2009) could be used to prevent injustice in relation to those who were not caught in the preceding provisions. In this case, it was held that such injustice would not occur because the separate inquest into the death of the applicant's son, Dodi Fayed, would have access to all the material available at the planned subsequent inquest into the death of Diana, Princess of Wales.

CHAPTER TWO

WHAT IS AN INQUEST?

WHAT IS AN INQUEST?

The word 'inquest' derives from the Old French '*enqueste*', meaning 'inquiry', and this remains an appropriate description in modern parlance. Under the 2009 Act a coroner is charged with conducting an investigation into violent, unexplained or unexpected deaths within their area. The inquest is an important and final part of that investigation.

PURPOSES OF AN INQUEST

BROAD PURPOSE – TO FIND THE TRUTH

An inquest is a fact-finding exercise; its broad purpose is to establish a set of key truths about a person's death. Most important for our purposes, and perhaps for those of the deceased's loved ones, is the question of how the person came about their death.

Unlike many other areas of law, an inquest does not have any power to determine questions of civil or criminal liability on the part of a named person (section 10(2) of the 2009 Act).

Given the nature of an inquest, it follows that an inquest is not a trial. It is often described as an inquisitorial rather than an adversarial process. Hence the commentary of the Divisional Court in *R (Thompson) v HM Coroner for South London* (1982) 126 SJ 625, The Times, 9 July 1982 Divisional Court, *per* Lord Lane CJ:

> "*An inquest is a fact finding exercise and not a method of apportioning guilt. The procedure and rules of evidence which are suitable for one are unsuitable for the other. In an inquest, it should never be forgotten that there are no parties, there is no indictment, there is no prosecution,*

there is no defence, there is no trial, simply an attempt to establish facts. It is an inquisitorial process, a process of investigation quite unlike a trial where the prosecutor accuses and the accused defends."

Whilst the comments of Lord Lane CJ in 1982 remain correct today, it is worth noting that the lines between adversarial and inquisitorial processes are now accepted to be more blurred in practice than was thought back then. The relatively more recent commentary of the House of Lords in *Middleton* (2004) 2 AC 182 made this clear at paragraph 26:

"26. … The 1984 Rules prescribe a hybrid procedure, not purely inquisitorial or purely adversarial. On the one hand, notice of the inquest must be given to the next-of-kin of the deceased and a widely defined group of other interested parties … who are entitled to examine witnesses either in person or by an authorised advocate … witnesses are privileged against self-incrimination; notice must be given to, and attendance facilitated of, persons whose conduct is likely to be called into question: …. On the other hand, the coroner calls and first examines all witnesses, the representative of a witness questioning him last … no person is allowed to address the coroner or the jury as to the facts … and there is no particularised charge or complaint as in criminal or civil proceedings. In addition to examining the witnesses the coroner … sums up the evidence to the jury and directs them as to the law …."

SPECIFIC PURPOSES – SECTION 5 OF THE 2009 ACT

Section 5 of the 2009 Act sets out the specific purposes of an inquest in modern coronial law:

"***5 Matters to be ascertained***

(1) The purpose of an investigation under this Part into a person's death is to ascertain—

(a) who the deceased was;

> *(b) how, when and where the deceased came by his or her death;*
>
> *(c) the particulars (if any) required by the 1953 Act to be registered concerning the death.*

(2) Where necessary in order to avoid a breach of any Convention rights (within the meaning of the Human Rights Act 1998 (c. 42)), the purpose mentioned in subsection (1)(b) is to be read as including the purpose of ascertaining in what circumstances the deceased came by his or her death.

(3) Neither the senior coroner conducting an investigation under this Part into a person's death nor the jury (if there is one) may express any opinion on any matter other than—

> *(a) the questions mentioned in subsection (1)(a) and (b) (read with subsection (2) where applicable);*
>
> *(b) the particulars mentioned in subsection (1)(c).*"

In addition to these purposes, the coroner also has a duty to identify systemic risks which may give rise to the possibility of such a death happening again, and to make recommendations to stop such a possibility. Those recommendations are encapsulated within a report to prevent future deaths (discussed in detail in Chapter 14).

Section 5 of the 2009 Act makes clear that the specific purposes of an investigation (and, therefore, an inquest) by a coroner are to ascertain:

(a) Who the deceased was;

(b) How, when and where the deceased came by his or her death;

(c) The particulars (if any) required by the 1953 Act to be registered concerning the death.

In practice, the majority of inquests will not need to concern themselves with conflicting evidence as to who the deceased was or when and where they came by their death. The main focus for the vast majority of inquests is the question of 'how' the deceased came by his or her death. Indeed, for practitioners, this will most likely be the key area of focus when acting in an inquest.

The scope of the evidence which the inquest will consider in answering this question will depend on whether the facts of that particular case require a *Jamieson* (otherwise known as a 'traditional') inquest or a *Middleton* (otherwise known as an 'Article 2') inquest. The nature of those inquests, and how the coroner determines which is appropriate in a given case, is a fairly large and complex subject and so is dealt with in some detail in chapter 6.

WHAT DOES THE INQUEST PROCESS LOOK LIKE?

Once the coroner has determined that an inquest needs to be held:

- The coroner must formally open the inquest as soon as reasonably practicable. This should be done in public;
- When the inquest is opened, the coroner will set a date for the inquest hearing or (if that is not possible) set a date for a pre-inquest review;
- If the case is one which would benefit from a pre-inquest review, then at least one pre-inquest review will be held in order to assist with case management;
- The inquest hearing takes place. This can take any form from an inquest relying entirely on written evidence with nobody present aside from the coroner right through to a large public hearing involving a coroner, jury, interested persons and advocates. Depending on the sort of hearing, the coroner may examine witnesses, receive other forms of evidence and take submissions on the law from advocates. In all inquests the coroner (or the jury,

if it is an inquest with a jury) will aim to reach a conclusion as to the cause of death;

- The coroner may, in appropriate circumstances, create a report for the prevention of future deaths which will be provided to those who the coroner considers can make meaningful changes. It may also be published online.

CHAPTER THREE

STARTING, STOPPING AND RESUMING AN INVESTIGATION

STARTING AN INVESTIGATION

In certain circumstances the Coroner has a duty to start an investigation into a death. In certain other circumstances the coroner has the power to start an investigation.

We shall consider each in turn.

DUTY TO START AN INVESTIGATION

Section 1 of the 2009 Act states (so far as relevant):

> "***1 Duty to investigate certain deaths***
>
> *(1) A senior coroner who is made aware that the body of a deceased person is within that coroner's area must as soon as practicable conduct an investigation into the person's death if subsection (2) applies.*
>
> *(2) This subsection applies if the coroner has reason to suspect that—*
>
> > *(a) the deceased died a violent or unnatural death,*
> >
> > *(b) the cause of death is unknown, or*
> >
> > *(c) the deceased died while in custody or otherwise in state detention.*"

Meaning of the word 'unnatural'

There have been some key cases which have assisted with the definition of the word 'unnatural'.

R (Touche) v Inner London North Coroner (2001) EWCA Civ 383

This was a case where the coroner appealed against the decision of the Divisional Court that he had erred in deciding not to hold an inquest into a woman's death. The deceased had suffered from a cerebral haemorrhage soon after giving birth in circumstances that suggested that, had her blood pressure been properly monitored immediately after the birth, her death might have been avoided. The coroner concluded that the deceased had suffered a natural death and no inquest was needed. The Divisional Court had found that he had erred in making this decision.

The Court of Appeal dismissed the coroner's appeal against the decision of the lower court. It held that the coroner ought to have held an inquest upon the receipt of information suggesting the possibility of 'neglect' in the deceased's treatment. Furthermore, *per curiam*, the Court held that otherwise natural deaths might be rendered unnatural by the fact that they are wholly unexpected. At 1219 *per* Brown LJ:

> "*Given our conclusion on the narrow point—that inquests should in any event be held into cases like this because of the possibility of a "neglect" verdict, the resolution of the wider point is clearly of less significance than it would otherwise be. Take, for example, the Divisional Court's example of Miss Thomas's attack having been relatively mild and the ambulance arriving quickly "but its journey to the hospital [having been] extended because the crew stopped for ten minutes at a public house, with the result that when she arrived at hospital her life could not be saved". I would regard such a case as falling comfortably into the "neglect" category: Miss Thomas on that scenario would already have been a dependent of an ambulance crew who then grossly failed in her care. But undoubtedly there will be cases which fall outside the category of "neglect" and yet appear to call for an*

> *inquest on the basis already indicated, namely, cases involving a wholly unexpected death from natural causes which would not have occurred but for some culpable human failure, a category of cases already perhaps recognised by the editors of Halsbury's Laws and Statutes. It is the combination of their unexpectedness and the culpable human failing that allowed them to happen which to my mind makes such deaths unnatural. Deaths by natural causes though undoubtedly they are, they should plainly never have happened and in that sense are unnatural."*

Note that the 'Miss Thomas' referred to here is in fact the deceased in the case below (*R v Poplar Coroner ex p Thomas*), as the Court undertook a detailed comparison with that case.

R v Poplar Coroner ex p Thomas (1993) QB 610

The Court of Appeal concluded that the word 'unnatural' should be given its ordinary meaning; the question of whether a death was natural or unnatural depended on the cause of death which was essentially a practical question of fact to be answered by ordinary common sense. Simon Brown LJ, at 388A, further explained that the circumstances surrounding the death may turn what might otherwise be a natural death into an unnatural one:

> *"I agree that unnatural is an ordinary word of the English language and that there is nothing to suggest that in s.8(1) of the Coroners Act 1988 it is being used in any unusual sense. That, however, is not to say that that whether or not a particular death is properly to be regarded as unnatural is a pure question of fact. On the contrary it seems to me that some guidance at least can and should be given as a matter of law by the Courts to Coroners ..."*

And at 389 C:

> *"... it seems to me necessary to recognise that cases may well arise in which human fault can and properly should be found to turn what would otherwise be a natural death into an un-natural one, and into which, therefore, an inquest should be held."*

R (Weeks) v South London Coroner (1996) EWHC Admin 329

The deceased was an insulin-dependent diabetic with heart problems who was resident in a nursing home. Following her death, the family raised a number of complaints with the local authority who conducted an investigation. That investigation was described by the Court as telling a "*lamentable tale of incompetence in the running of the home*".

However, the coroner considered that the death "*appeared to be a natural one registered by a medical practitioner*" and further considered that the deceased's daughter's complaints were not matters for the inquest. In a later letter the coroner made clear that "*unless it was suggested that the doctor was guilty of some malpractice he was bound to accept the cause of death because there was no possibility of holding a post mortem*".

The family judicially reviewed the coroner's decision that he had no duty to hold an inquest. On judicial review, *per* Scott Baker LJ:

> "*...when a Coroner is informed of a death within his jurisdiction, he must consider all the relevant material before him and ask whether he has reasonable cause to suspect that the deceased died a violent or unnatural death or a sudden death the cause of which is unknown. If he does have cause to suspect, he must hold an inquest. The test is one of objective fact. The matters that fall to be considered are not limited to admissible evidence*".

The Court found that in the circumstances of this case there was nothing to suggest either that the death was unnatural or that it was a sudden death of which the cause was unknown.

Scott Baker LJ did add, though:

> "*Even were I to have reached a different conclusion I would have found it difficult to exercise my discretion to grant the relief sought. There was an exhaustive investigation into what happened in the home at the material time. Serious deficiencies were exposed. Later there was a hearing before a Panel chaired by an independent social worker. If an*

inquest were now to be held it would take place 3 years after the death. In the absence of a post mortem and in the light of the very extensive investigations that have already taken place it is doubtful if anything new would be learned."

Meaning of 'reasonable cause to suspect'

<u>Canning v Northants Coroner (2005) EWHC 3125 (Admin)</u>

'Reasonable cause to suspect' denotes a low threshold as made clear in paragraph 3 of this case, *per* Carnwath LJ:

> "*The words 'reasonable cause to suspect' imply a low threshold. They do not require a prima facie case; see Hussein v Choung Fook Kam (1970) AC 942. Finally, the coroner's decision not to hold an inquest can only be impugned on Wednesbury grounds, in other words for irrationality or illegality*".

POWER TO START AN INVESTIGATION

Sections 1(4) and (5) of the 2009 Act provide:

> "*(4) A senior coroner who has reason to believe that—*
>
> *(a) a death has occurred in or near the coroner's area,*
>
> *(b) the circumstances of the death are such that there should be an investigation into it, and*
>
> *(c) the duty to conduct an investigation into the death under subsection (1) does not arise because of the destruction, loss or absence of the body,*
>
> *may report the matter to the Chief Coroner.*
>
> *(5) On receiving a report under subsection (4) the Chief Coroner may direct a senior coroner (who does not have to be the one who made the report) to conduct an investigation into the death."*

Therefore, where the senior coroner has reason to believe that:

1. A death has occurred in or near the coroner's area;
2. The circumstances of the death are such that there should be an investigation into it; and
3. The body has been destroyed, lost or is otherwise absent which means that the duty to conduct an investigation under section of 1(1) CAJA 2009 does not arise

Then there is a power to investigate.

In those circumstances the senior coroner may report the matter to the Chief Coroner, who then has discretion to direct that an inquest takes place. If that direction is given, the investigation must take place as soon as practicable.

The power to investigate under sections 1(4) and (5) CAJA 2009 may arise if, for example, the senior coroner is not informed of the existence of the body until after it has been removed from his/her area, if it has been buried or cremated or where the body has disappeared.

The senior coroner has the power to make whatever enquiries appear necessary to decide whether the duty and power in section 1 arises (section 1(7) of CAJA 2009)

STOPPING AN INVESTIGATION

Schedule 1 of the 2009 Act deals with the suspension and resumption of investigations.

Where an investigation is suspended, the coroner must adjourn any inquest that is being held as part of the investigation. If the inquest is held with a jury, then the coroner may discharge the jury (see paragraph 6 of Schedule 1 to the 2009 Act).

Schedule 1 of the 2009 Act contains specific duties to suspend an investigation and a general power to do so.

Paragraph 1 duty: a person may be charged with a homicide offence involving the death of the deceased or an offence that is alleged to be a related offence

The first duty to suspend is where a prosecuting authority (such as the Crown Prosecution Service) requests the coroner to suspend the investigation because a person may be charged with an offence in relation to the death of the deceased which, broadly speaking, can be said to make them culpable for the death. That duty is set out in paragraph 1 of Schedule 1 to the 2009 Act.

> "*(1) A senior coroner must suspend an investigation under this Part of this Act into a person's death in the following cases.*
>
> *(2) The first case is where a prosecuting authority requests the coroner to suspend the investigation on the ground that a person may be charged with—*
>
>> *(a) a homicide offence involving the death of the deceased, or*
>>
>> *(b) an offence (other than a service offence) that is alleged to be a related offence.*"

Sub-paragraph 3 has equivalent provisions for service offences.

'Homicide offence' is defined in para 1(6) of Schedule 1 to the CAJA 2009 as murder, manslaughter, corporate manslaughter, infanticide and certain other offences involving death by driving, encouraging or assisting suicide and causing or allowing the death of a child or vulnerable adult. Within that same paragraph, 'related offence' is defined as an offence that involves a death.

Under paragraph 1(4) of Schedule 1 to the 2009 act, a suspension must be for:

"*(a) a period of 28 days beginning with the day on which the suspension first takes effect, or*

(b) whatever longer period (beginning with that day) the coroner specifies."

Under paragraph 1(5) of Schedule 1 to the 2009 Act the period referred to in paragraph 1(4) may be extended, or further extended, at the request of the authority by whom the suspension was originally requested.

Paragraph 2 duty: a person has been charged with a homicide offence or a related offence

The second duty to suspend is where a person has appeared before a magistrates' court or been charged on an indictment in relation to a homicide offence involving the death of the deceased. If the coroner either becomes aware that this has happened, or is specifically requested by the prosecuting authority to suspend the coronial investigation because this has happened, then the coroner is under a duty to suspend.

"*(1) Subject to sub-paragraph (6), a senior coroner must suspend an investigation under this Part of this Act into a person's death in the following cases.*

(2) The first case is where the coroner—

(a) becomes aware that a person has appeared or been brought before a magistrates' court charged with a homicide offence involving the death of the deceased, or

(b) becomes aware that a person has been charged on an indictment with such an offence without having appeared or been brought before a magistrates' court charged with it.

(3) The second case is where the coroner becomes aware that a person has been charged with the service equivalent of a homicide offence involving the death of the deceased.

(4) The third case is where a prosecuting authority informs the coroner that a person—

(a) has appeared or been brought before a magistrates' court charged with an offence (other than a service offence) that is alleged to be a related offence, or

(b) has been charged on an indictment with such an offence without having been sent for trial for it,

and the prosecuting authority requests the coroner to suspend the investigation.

(5) The fourth case is where the Director of Service Prosecutions informs the coroner that a person has been charged with a service offence that is alleged to be a related offence, and the Director requests the coroner to suspend the investigation."

This duty, however, is subject to paragraph 2(6) of Schedule 1 to the 2009 Act, which provides that the coroner need not suspend the investigation if:

a) The prosecuting authority informs the coroner that it has no objection to the investigation continuing (in the first case – the coroner becoming aware of the appearance/charge);

b) The Director of Service Prosecutions informs the coroner that s/he has no objection to the investigation continuing (in the second case – the prosecuting authority requesting the coroner to suspend the investigation due to appearance/charge); or

c) If the coroner thinks there is an exceptional reason for not suspending the investigation (in any case).

Paragraph 3 duty: public inquiries

> "*(1) Subject to sub-paragraph (2), a senior coroner must suspend an investigation under this Part of this Act into a person's death if—*
>
> > *(a) the Lord Chancellor requests the coroner to do so on the ground that the cause of death is likely to be adequately investigated by an inquiry under the Inquiries Act 2005 (c. 12) that is being or is to be held,*
> >
> > *(b) a senior judge has been appointed under that Act as chairman of the inquiry, and*
> >
> > *(c) the Lord Chief Justice has indicated approval to the Lord Chancellor, for the purposes of this paragraph, of the appointment of that judge.*
>
> *In paragraph (b) "senior judge" means a judge of the High Court or the Court of Appeal or a Justice of the Supreme Court.*"

However, this duty is subject to paragraph 3(2):

> "*(2) The coroner need not suspend the investigation if there appears to be an exceptional reason for not doing so.*"

Paragraph 4 adds an additional qualifier to the duty under paragraph 3:

> "*(1) This paragraph applies where an investigation is suspended under paragraph 3 on the basis that the cause of death is likely to be adequately investigated by an inquiry under the Inquiries Act 2005 (c. 12).*
>
> *(2) The terms of reference of the inquiry must be such that it has as its purpose, or among its purposes, the purpose set out in section 5(1) above (read with section 5(2) where applicable); and section 5 of the Inquiries Act 2005 has effect accordingly.*"

Therefore the statute ensures that the inquest purposes are still met if the inquest is suspended in favour of a public inquiry. In this way, the inquest is effectively subsumed by the inquiry.

In practice, the coroner in charge of the inquest may well be appointed to be Chair of the Inquiry – for example, in 2012 Sir Robert Owen was appointed to conduct the inquest into the death of Alexander Litvinienko. Sir Owen petitioned the Home Secretary to set up an inquiry into his death so that certain sensitive issues of national security could be explored properly. Accordingly the Litvinienko Inquiry was formally set up on 31 July 2014, and Sir Robert Owen appointed as its Chair[5].

Paragraph 5 power: coroner's discretion

Finally, paragraph 5 of Schedule 1 of the CAJA 2009 contains a catch-all power to suspend an investigation when the coroner considers it 'appropriate' to do so:

> "*A senior coroner may suspend an investigation under this Part of this Act into a person's death in any case if it appears to the coroner that it would be appropriate to do so.*"

The coroner is therefore afforded a wide measure of discretion in determining whether an inquest should be suspended – a theme which is repeated throughout the legislation.

Rule 25 of the 2013 Rules: power to adjourn

The coroner also has fairly wide discretion to adjourn an inquest if he or she considers it reasonable to do so:

---

[5] See part 2 of *The Litvinienko Inquiry: Report into the death of Alexander Litvinienko*, Chairman: Sir Robert Owen, January 2016, available at https://assets.publishing.service.gov.uk/media/5a8055c340f0b62302692e48/The-Litvinenko-Inquiry-H-C-695-web.pdf, last accessed on 4 October 2023.

"25.— Adjournment and resumption of an inquest

(1) A coroner may adjourn an inquest if the coroner is of the view that it is reasonable to do so.

(2) The coroner must inform the next of kin or personal representative of the deceased and any other interested persons who have made themselves known to the coroner as soon as reasonably practicable of the decision to adjourn, the date of the decision to adjourn and the reason for the adjournment.

(3) The coroner must inform the next of kin or personal representative of the deceased and any other interested persons who have made themselves known to the coroner as soon as reasonably practicable of the date, time and place at which an adjourned inquest is to be resumed.

(4) A coroner must adjourn an inquest and notify the Director of Public Prosecutions, if during the course of the inquest, it appears to the coroner that the death of the deceased is likely to have been due to a homicide offence and that a person may be charged in relation to the offence."

As an example of when an adjournment may be reasonable, see *R v HM Coroner for Kent (Maidstone District) ex p Johnstone* (1994) 6 WLUK 273. In that case the deceased was a schizophrenic who was being treated with neuroleptic drugs. He died following his collapse while an inpatient at Maidstone Hospital. The post-mortem gave the cause of death as "neuroleptic malignant syndrome", leading the family to believe that he had died from a reaction to the drugs. At the inquest, the cause of death was stated as being "acute exhaustive mania", and that neuroleptic drugs played no part in causing the death. The family requested an adjournment to obtain further medical evidence, which was refused and a verdict of death due to natural causes. In granting the family's application for judicial review of the decision not to adjourn, the High Court held that where a family was misled as to the cause of death, an adjournment should be granted. Further medical evidence was required and failure to obtain it amounted to insufficiency of enquiry.

Rule 25(4) does not mean that a coroner cannot leave a conclusion of unlawful killing to a jury unless s/he has first referred the matter to the DPP. After all, the test for leaving a conclusion of unlawful killing to a jury is different than the test for referral. The former is simply that there is evidence upon which a reasonable jury could reach the unlawful killing conclusion and it would be safe to leave it to the jury (see chapter 12). The latter has echoes of the civil standard of proof in using the language 'is likely to have been'. In addition, the section requires that a person can be identified as responsible to the point of being likely to be charged in criminal proceedings. That has echoes of the standard of criminal charge, which at the Crown Prosecution Service level is that there is a realistic prospect of conviction and it is in the public interest to charge. It is accordingly, again, a different standard from the comparatively low threshold required to leave a conclusion of unlawful killing to a jury.

This does make sense; a referral to the Director of Public Prosecutions would almost inevitably lead to the inquest jury (if one is empanelled) being discharged while they consider the issue. It would not stand to reason that Parliament would have intended such a disruptive effect to happen automatically in any case where 'unlawful killing' is likely to be left to the jury as a conclusion.

RESUMING AN INVESTIGATION

Paragraphs 7 to 10 of Schedule 1 to the 2009 Act deal with resumption of an inquest that has been suspended in the above circumstances.

Paragraph 7 deals with Paragraph 1 duty to suspend

Paragraph 7 provides grounds for resumption in relation to an investigation suspended under paragraph 1 (i.e. suspension on the basis that a person may be charged with a homicide or related offence). An investigation suspended under paragraph 1 must be resumed once the period of suspension (as specified in that section) has lapsed.

Paragraph 8 deals with the Paragraph 2 duty to suspend

The paragraph 2 duty arises where a person appears before a Magistrates' Court, or is charged on indictment with, a homicide offence. Paragraph 8 says that an investigation suspended under paragraph 2 may not be resumed unless – but must be resumed if – the senior coroner thinks that there is sufficient reason for resuming it.

If the investigation is resumed under this paragraph, the inquest's determination cannot be inconsistent with the criminal proceedings for which the investigation was suspended under Paragraph 2. For example, if a person was found guilty of murder in the criminal proceedings, the inquest cannot then determine that the death was caused by 'accident' or 'natural causes', which would patently be inconsistent with the verdict of the criminal court.

Paragraph 9 deals with the Paragraph 3 duty to suspend

Paragraph 3 is the duty to suspend where there is a public inquiry which, effectively, subsumes the inquest. In a similar way to paragraph 8, paragraph 9 provides that an investigation suspended under paragraph 3 may not be resumed unless – but must be resumed if – the coroner thinks there is sufficient reason for so doing.

Paragraph 10 deals with the Paragraph 5 power to suspend

Paragraph 5 gives the coroner the power to suspend an investigation where it appears 'appropriate' to do so. Paragraph 10 provides that an investigation suspended under paragraph 5 may be resumed at any time if "*the senior coroner thinks that there is sufficient reason for resuming it*".

Where there remain questions that other available investigative mechanisms have not been able to address, it seems that this will be a ground for resuming an inquest under paragraph 10. All that the coroner needs to be satisfied of is that there are real questions requiring investigation, rather than that there is clear evidence of wrongdoing or the like. So in *R(Moss) v HM Coroner for Durham and Darlington* (2008) EWHC 2940, the High Court quashed the coroner's decision not to resume an inquest, saying:

> "... *it is impossible to know from the contents of the statements provided whether there is in fact any real ground for criticism of the failure to take any more effective action about Dr Martin's perceived deficiencies or whether that failure contributed in any sufficiently direct way to Mr Moss' death. But that cuts both ways. Mr Cragg is entitled to say that it is precisely because so little has yet been established that an inquest is necessary: all that the Claimant needs to do is to establish that there is a real question which requires investigation.*"

By contrast, in *Fraser v North West Wales Coroner* (2010) EWHC 1165 (admin) the court refused to quash the coroner's decision not to resume an inquest after a criminal trial. In that case the purpose of resuming the inquest was to correct the cause of death on the register; this was not sufficient reason to resume the inquest. There would be no new evidence, and it was clear that the new inquest would not reach any different conclusion on the facts.

PART TWO

FROM INSTRUCTION TO HEARING (PRE-INQUEST MATTERS)

CHAPTER FOUR

FORMALLY OPENING AN INQUEST

WHEN IS AN INQUEST OPENED?

It may seem odd to those of us who have practised in other areas that the coroner will open the inquest formally before being ready to conduct the hearing as a whole. Unlike in, for example, criminal trials, the inquest will be formally opened and then a later date set for either the inquest hearing or the pre-inquest review.

Why open an inquest in this way? Once opened, an inquest must be concluded (paragraph 47 of the Chief Coroner's Guidance No.9 *Opening an Inquest*). At the inquest hearing a date is set for either the substantive hearing or a pre-inquest review. Given that an inquest must be opened as soon as reasonably practicable after the coroner has determined that the duty to hold an inquest applies, this means that there is less risk of an inquest simply languishing for an unspecified period of time which would be highly unsatisfactory. In addition, proceedings become 'active' for contempt of court purposes once an inquest has been opened (para 45 of the Guidance).

When a coroner has determined that the duty to hold an inquest applies, the coroner must open that inquest as soon as reasonably practicable, under Rule 5(1) of the Coroners (Inquests) Rules 2013.

The Guidance says, at para 9, that although there is no rule to the effect that the family of the deceased should be notified of the time, date and place of the opening in all cases it is good practice to do so. It may also be good practice to notify others who appear at that stage to be likely to have an interest in the proceedings.

INQUEST TO BE OPENED IN PUBLIC

Under Rule 11(1) of the Coroners (Inquest) Rules 2013 the coroner must open an inquest in public:

> "***11.— Inquest hearings to be held in public***
>
> *(1) A coroner must open an inquest in public.*
>
> *(2) Where the coroner does not have immediate access to a court room or other appropriate premises, the coroner may open the inquest privately and then announce that the inquest has been opened at the next inquest hearing held in public.*"

The Guidance indicates that the criteria for opening the inquest privately under section 11(2) is that there would be "unavoidable delay in applying rule 11(1), for example in some jurisdictions where no court or room used as a court is readily available".

The Guidance makes clear at paragraph 14 that "*coroners should not fall back on rule 11(2) as an easy excuse for not opening in public. Where court logistics are difficult, they should encourage the local authority to be more helpful in providing a court space. And in any event there should be less need for this procedure now that the body can be released without opening an inquest. It goes without saying that the principle of open justice is a long-standing and important tenet of constitutional law.*"

Under Rule 5(2) of the 2013 Inquest Rules, at the opening hearing the coroner must either set the date for the inquest of set the date for a pre-inquest review hearing.

Under Rule 8 of the 2013 Inquest Rules the coroner has a duty to complete the inquest within six months of notification of the death where possible. As a result, the Guidance indicates at paragraph 27 that the date for the inquest must normally be set within six months of the date on which the coroner is made aware of the death. Where there is good reason for not so doing, Rule 8 still bestows a duty on the coroner to complete the inquest as soon as is reasonably practicable after the date of notification of the death.

Para 29 of the Guidance indicates that if there is likely to be such a delay, the coroner should fix a date within a reasonable time for a pre-inquest review hearing (see chapter five). The Coroner should also state what it is intended should be achieved at that hearing (paragraph 30 of the Guidance).

In addition to fixing a date, the coroner should give directions, when feasible, including a timetable for the provision of reports and statements, especially those of a medical nature (paragraph 35 of the Guidance). The Guidance indicates that in the normal course of events, with the duty to hear and complete inquests within six months, the coroner should direct that specific reports and statements should be provided within three weeks.

PUBLISICING THE OPENING OF AN INQUEST

As noted above, an inquest must be opened in public subject to limited exception. It follows that the coroner must make the details of the opening public where possible.

The Guidance indicates, at paragraphs 40 to 41, that the coroner is required to make details of all final inquest hearings public, and preferably by way of publication on a website. At paragraph 42, the Guidance states that where possible the same practice should apply to each opening (although not if it will cause delay) and pre-inquest review hearings, adding:

> "*If the hearing is in public and the public (including the press) have a right to attend, that right is of no value unless notice of the hearing is made publicly available in advance.*"

SUMMARY

In summary, then:

- Once the coroner is aware of the duty to hold an inquest, that inquest must be opened as soon as reasonably practicable;
- The family must be notified in advance;
- Others should be notified where possible;
- Notice of the opening should be published where possible;
- The inquest should be opened in public unless the exception applies;
- The opening must be recorded;
- Identification evidence should be received;
- The date for an inquest or pre-inquest review should be set;
- Directions should be made as to timetable of reports and the like.

CHAPTER FIVE

PRE-INQUEST REVIEWS

WHAT IS A PRE-INQUEST REVIEW?

As the name suggests, a pre-inquest review is a hearing held before the inquest hearing in order to iron out any issues relating to the conduct of the inquest. Before the 2009 Act and 2013 Inquest Rules, pre-inquest reviews (or "PIRs") were held, if at all, without any formal footing in statute. Instead, they were something which a coroner might decide to convene if they considered that the case was of such a nature as to warrant discussions with the interested persons before the day of the inquest hearing.

That changed after 25 July 2013. Pre-inquest reviews were now formalised by virtue of Rule 6 of the 2013 Inquests Rules:

> "*A coroner may at any time during the course of an investigation and before an inquest hearing hold a pre-inquest review hearing.*"

In addition, the Chief Coroner issued Guidance No.22 on 18 January 2016, which is a useful guide to the conduct of pre-inquest reviews for coroners and practitioners alike.

WHEN WILL THERE BE A PRE-INQUEST REVIEW?

Guidance No.22 states, at paragraph 2:

> "*PIRs should be held in more complex investigations where there is a need for issues to be aired prior to the inquest and which cannot easily be dealt with by email*".

There is no diktat as to when a case becomes complex enough that a pre-inquest review should be held; that would appear to be a question left to the judgment of the coroner. It does make the most sense for the coroner – who has the best knowledge of the investigation and is responsible for conducting it to the end – to determine whether they need to air any issues in advance.

PURPOSES OF A PRE-INQUEST REVIEW

Guidance Sheet No.22 sets out the broad purpose of the pre-inquest review at paragraph 3:

> "*The purpose of a PIR is to ensure that the case is managed effectively, efficiently and openly. Before the 2013 Rules were introduced, it was intended that PIRs should provide the opportunity for the scope, issues and conduct of an inquest to be stablished. Families and other participants could raise issues, particularly contentious issues, on these and other key topics so that surprises could be avoided.*"

Specifically, it may be said that the purposes of a pre-inquest review are as follows:

- To keep control of the disclosure process;
- To ensure smooth running of the final inquest by having legal arguments in advance;
- To identify any particular issues or themes of concern;
- To get the evidence in order.

WHAT DOES A PRE-INQUEST REVIEW LOOK LIKE?

A pre-inquest review is, much like the final inquest hearing, led by the coroner. It is a public hearing at which the coroner and those representing the interested persons (or the interested persons themselves if unrepresented) will be present. Nobody else is required, but they are generally able to attend in the same way that they may attend the final inquest hearing.

The pre-inquest review is usually relatively informal, notwithstanding that there may be legal arguments and rulings.

At paragraph 4 of Guidance Sheet No.22, the Chief Coroner recommends:

> "*Normally there should only be one PIR, although there may be more when necessary. PIRs should not, however, be used in the guise of regular 'mention' hearings, for which there should be no justifiable need*".

At paragraph 5 of Guidance Sheet No.22 the Chief Coroner sets out what is referred to as the 'three essential elements' of the pre-inquest review:

> "*The three essential elements of a PIR are:*
>
> *(1) An agenda in advance*
>
> *(2) The hearing*
>
> *(3) Rulings (with reasons)*".

An agenda in advance

Paragraph 14 of Guidance Sheet No.22 indicates that all interested persons should have the agenda and sufficient disclosure well in advance. Paragraph 6 indicates that the agenda should be sent out at least 14 days in advance wherever possible.

Paragraph 10 provides some more detail:

> "*The coroner should ensure that Interested Persons, particularly those unrepresented, have sufficient disclosure of relevant statements and documents before a PIR so that they can address the agenda on an informed basis. For example, Interested Persons should not be placed*

> *in the position of having to discuss a witness list without having received any witness statements, although in some cases it may be necessary to hold an early PIR in order to manage effectively the future disclosure of materials by Interested Persons.*"

In Brown v HM Coroner for Norfolk (2014) EWHC 187, which pre-dates the Chief Coroner's Guidance No.22 and is referenced in that Guidance, the High Court gave its own guidance on the handling of pre-inquest review hearings. Paragraphs 39 to 41 make clear the importance of giving interested persons advance notice of the agenda items:

> "*39. A pre-inquest review hearing, where held, is an important stage towards the final hearing. In each case the coroner should ensure that all interested persons, particularly bereaved families, have sufficient notice of the matters to be discussed at the pre-inquest review hearing. The claimant asserted in this case that he had no notice of what was going to be discussed at the hearing and was therefore unprepared when asked which witnesses should attend to give evidence and whether he accepted that the cause of death could not be established. Coroners should therefore provide a written agenda in advance and, if appropriate, express provisional views so that agreement or opposition can be expressed.*
>
> *40. The agenda which should be tailored to the individual case should include, amongst other things, and particularly in the more complex or difficult cases, a list of interested persons, a proposed list of witnesses identifying those who may be called and those whose statements may be read, the issues to be considered at the inquest, the scope of the evidence, whether a jury will be required, whether Article 2 of the European Convention on Human Rights is engaged, any issues of disclosure, the date of the final hearing, and any other relevant matters. In a complex or difficult investigation interested persons should be invited to respond to the coroner's agenda in advance of the pre-inquest review hearing in writing, stating what they agree with and what they do not agree with.*

> *41. The coroner should also ensure that interested persons, particularly those unrepresented, have sufficient disclosure of relevant statements and documents before the pre-inquest review hearing so as to be able to address the agenda on an informed basis. The claimant asserted in this case, as the coroner's note of the hearing states, that 'he had not received copies of the post mortem and toxicology reports'. If correct, that would have placed him at a considerable disadvantage for the pre-inquest review hearing."*

Paragraph 9 of the Guidance Sheet No.22 adds that in some cases it may be helpful if the coroner sets out a provisional view on one or more items on the agenda:

> *"If the coroner is able to indicate a provisional view, especially on an issue which is unlikely to be hotly contested, it should be made clear that this is an indication only and no final decision has yet been made. A provisional view gives Interested Persons the opportunity to consider the issues in advance of the hearing. In an appropriate case they should be invited to respond to the agenda in advance in writing, expressing agreement or opposition."*

The guidance gives an example as follows:

> *"My provisional view, subject to representations, is that a jury may be required. Applying the low threshold test, there is reason to suspect that the death resulted from an omission of a police officer: see section 7(2)(b)(i), Coroners and Justice Act 2009. Alternatively, if the threshold test is not met, I may be minded to exercise my discretion under section 7(3). The family have asked for a jury and the facts bear a resemblance to the mandatory provisions in section 7(2)(b)(i) such that I may have 'sufficient reason' to summon a jury ...*
>
> *[...]*
>
> *But these are only provisional views, not final views. I would like to hear what Interested Persons have to say before I make any decisions."*

By virtue of paragraph 13, where possible the press should also be notified in advance of any non-factual issue likely to be of particular interest to them. One example might be where there are applications for anonymity of the witness.

The format of the hearing

We shall consider the content of discussions at the hearing separately – under the heading *What might be on the agenda?* Below and – in certain more complex cases – within their own chapters.

Guidance No.22 does, though, assist us with the way that a pre-inquest review hearing will be conducted. The main points to note are:

- Where possible, video-conferencing or telephone conferencing should be made available at pre-inquest reviews for those who wish to use it (paragraph 15);
- No evidence should be called at a pre-inquest review and no witness should be asked or required to attend. The coroner should take care not to appear to be expressing a view about any aspect of the evidence which will be the subject of decision at the inquest (paragraph 16);
- The hearing should follow the agenda, subject to late amendments or additions (paragraph 17);
- The hearing must ordinarily be held in public by virtue of Rule 11(3) of the 2013 Inquests Rules. The coroner may, though, direct that the public (but not interested persons) be excluded from a pre-inquest review if the coroner considers that it would be in the interests of justice or national security, by virtue of Rule 11(5) of the 2013 Inquests Rules (paragraph 18);
- The pre-inquest review must be recorded and the recording kept by virtue of Rule 26 of the 2013 Inquests Rules (paragraph 19).

Rulings (with reasons)

Where there are legal matters to be resolved before the inquest begins, they will almost certainly be raised at the pre-inquest review(s). Whether or not the interested persons agree on the issue, the coroner will make the ultimate decision.

Where a decision is required, the coroner should give a clear, brief ruling at the pre-inquest review. Of course, sometimes the coroner may require time to consider their decision. If that is the case then the coroner should provide his or her ruling within seven working days of the hearing (paragraph 20 of Guidance No.22).

The ruling may not be provided at the hearing in writing – but after the hearing, all the coroner's decisions should be summarised in writing so that they can be circulated to interested persons (paragraph 21 of Guidance No.22).

Any ruling on a contested issue should be accompanied by reasons justifying the coroner's decision, albeit they can be brief. Reasons may be unnecessary where there is agreement between interested persons and for most 'housekeeping' decisions (paragraph 22 of Guidance No.22).

WHAT MIGHT BE ON THE AGENDA OF A PRE-INQUEST REVIEW?

Paragraphs 7 and 8 of Guidance No.22 list the items which may be on the agenda for a pre-inquest review. They include the following:

- Scope of the inquest / whether Article 2 is engaged;
- Whether there will be a jury;
- Identity of interested persons and/or witnesses;
- The evidence to be called;

- Applications on behalf of witnesses (e.g. special measures, anonymity);
- Practicalities (e.g. date of the next pre-inquest review hearing, date of the inquest, length of the inquest);
- Whether there should be counsel to the inquest.

SCOPE OF THE INQUEST (WHETHER ARTICLE 2 IS ENGAGED)

'Scope' is such a large topic that we will deal with it in its own chapter (see Chapter 6). The coroner will be determining whether the question for the inquest in deciding 'how' the deceased came by his or her death will mean simply 'by what means' or whether it will be extended to include 'and in what circumstances'.

WHETHER A JURY WILL BE REQUIRED

Again, this is a fairly large topic and so will be dealt with in its own chapter (see Chapter 7). To some extent, this will be linked to the coroner's determination on the nature and scope of the inquest.

IDENTIFICATION OF INTERESTED PERSONS AND/OR WITNESSES

We have been through what an interested person is in some detail (see chapter 1 for discussion and caselaw).

Why might 'identification of interested persons' make its way onto the agenda? The pre-inquest review may be held fairly early on in the process; indeed, with a large inquest there may be a few pre-inquest reviews. At that early stage, the coroner may not have identified all of the interested persons. For example, the family may be aware of someone who they consider does fall into the category of 'interested person'. Equally, an individual or organisation aware of the inquest may wish to apply to the coroner for 'interested person' status.

On a similar note, at a pre-inquest review there may also be discussion about witnesses.

The Coroner has power to summon witnesses and compel the production of evidence under schedule 5, para 1 of CAJA 2009. If a witness does not attend an inquest having been summonsed, they may be committed for contempt of court under the case law (*HM Coroner for Kent v Terrill* (2000) Inquest LR 16). There are also various offences relating to witnesses and evidence created by Schedule 6 to the CAJA 2009.

The Coroner has wide discretion to decide which witnesses to call (*R(Mack) v HM Coroner for Birmingham & Solihull* (2011) EWCA Civ 712) but remember they of course are under a duty to undertake a proper inquiry into the relevant issues.

As a practitioner, your client may have given you instructions that there are others who should be called as witnesses. You need to consider whether and to what extent they will assist the coroner in undertaking a proper inquiry into the relevant issues. The pre-inquest review will therefore be the appropriate time to raise these potential witnesses with the coroner.

Interested persons may also wish to persuade the Coroner to call expert evidence. There is no right to call an expert witness, even in an Article 2 inquest. All must depend on the facts of the particular case. In *R(Goodson) v Bedfordshire and Luton Coroner* (2004) EWHC 1931 (Admin) at paragraph 71:

> *"71. As to effectiveness, the lack of independent expert evidence or review was certainly one of the reasons why the inquest in R (Wright) v Secretary of State for the Home Department [2001] UKHRR 1399, a case of death in custody, was held not to have been an effective investigation. The same is true of R (Nicholls) v Liverpool City Coroner [2001] EWHC Admin 922, another case of death in custody, though it had the particular feature that the deceased's family had instructed a medical expert whose report contained adverse comment*

on the standard of care received by the deceased but whom the coroner refused without good reason to call as a witness. So too in R (Stanley) v Inner North London Coroner [2003] EWHC 1180 (Admin), a case concerning the use of fatal force by police officers, the coroner's failure to call relevant experts who were present at the inquiry, including one funded by the family of the deceased, was held to be one of the reasons why the inquest was flawed. But each of those cases was decided on its own particular facts. None of them purported to lay down any principle that independent expert evidence is always required in order to render an inquest an effective investigation for the purposes of article 2. And in my view there can be no such principle. Everything must depend on the particular circumstances, including the expertise of the coroner himself and the precise nature of the issues and evidence before him."

The interested person who seeks to persuade the coroner to call expert evidence should identify the witness and the substance of the evidence which they may be able to give, so that the coroner can decide whether or not it is appropriate to call them (*R(Takoushis) v HM Coroner for Inner North London* (2005) EWCA Civ 1440). In *Takoushis* at paragraph 61:

"61. As to expert evidence, if an interested person wishes a coroner to call expert evidence in any particular case, it is for that person (if at all possible) to identify the witness and put the substance of the evidence which the witness may be able to give before the coroner so that the coroner may be able to decide whether or not it is appropriate."

Discussions at this stage may be as detailed as determining exactly which parts of an expert's report may and may not be aired in open court during the inquest hearing.

EVIDENCE TO BE CALLED AND DISCLOSURE

This is, again, a large enough topic that it is dealt with in a separate chapter (see chapter 8).

APPLICATIONS ON BEHALF OF WITNESSES (SPECIAL MEASURES)

Giving evidence by video link

By virtue of Rule 17 of the 2013 Inquests Rules the coroner may direct that a witness may give evidence at an inquest hearing through a live video link. This can only be given where the coroner determines that giving evidence by video link would improve the quality of the evidence given by the witness, or allow the inquest to proceed more expediently.

Before granting such an application, however, the coroner is enjoined to consider all the circumstances of the case, including a) any views expressed by the witness or any interested person; b) whether it would be in the interests of justice or national security to give evidence by video link; and c) whether in the opinion of the coroner, giving evidence by video link would impede the effectiveness of the questioning of the witnesses.

A direction may be given under this section on application by the witness (or their parent or legal guardian if they are a child), on application by interested person or on the coroner's own initiative.

Giving evidence from behind a screen

Under Rule 18 of the 2013 Inquests Rules the coroner may direct that a witness gives their evidence from behind a screen. The test for so doing is that the coroner decides this would be likely to improve the quality of the witness' evidence, or it is in the interests of justice or national security.

Before granting such an application, however, the coroner is enjoined to consider all the circumstances of the case, including a) any views expressed by the witness or any interested person; b) whether it would be in the interests of justice or national security to give evidence by video link; and c) whether in the opinion of the coroner, giving evidence by video link would impede the effectiveness of the questioning of the witnesses.

A direction may be given under this section on application by the witness (or their parent or legal guardian if they are a child), on application by interested person or on the coroner's own initiative.

Anonymity

The starting point is that pre-inquest and inquest hearings will be held in public (Rule 11(3) of the 2013 Inquests Rules). Under Rule 11(4) and 11(5), the coroner may direct that the public be excluded from either if considers that it is in the interests of:

a) National security; or

b) Justice

Note that, however, when the public is excluded that does not include the exclusion of interested persons, who can remain.

In certain circumstances a witness may make an application to the coroner for anonymity in the proceedings. Where these applications are made, they will be under human rights and/or common law umbrellas.

Under Rule 11 of the 2013 Inquests Rules the application will be heard in public, unless the 11(4) or 11(5) exceptions apply. (Note that Chief Coroner's Guidance No.25 *Coroners and the Media* states categorically, at paragraph 17, that applications for anonymity or screening of witnesses will be heard in public, but it would be extremely unlikely that the interests of national security or justice are disregarded in favour of the non-statutory guidance).

Inquests are subject to the Contempt of Court Act 1981. By section 11 of that Act, where the court allows a name or other matter to be withheld from the public in proceedings before the court, the court may give such directions prohibiting the publication of that name or matter in connection with proceedings as appears to the court to be necessary for the purpose for which it was so withheld. It is clear, then, that the media may well be interested in any application for anonymity.

With that in mind, paragraph 18 of Chief Coroner's Guidance No.25 *Coroners and the Media* provides:

> "*18. Where possible (a) any consideration of excluding the public from a hearing, or (b) any application for anonymity or screening of witnesses, or (c) the possible imposition of reporting restrictions (see below) should be addressed in advance at a PIR hearing, with due notice to the media. This gives the opportunity for the press to make representations should they wish. It also avoids late applications by the media at the inquest which the coroner may find disruptive.*"

The most common human rights grounds under which applications for anonymity will be made are: Article 2 (protection of the right to life) and Article 8 (the right to respect for private and family life).

Conversely, the media may be relying on Article 10 (the right to freedom of expression).

All of these rights may be infringed upon in particular circumstances. Note, though, that Article 2 may only be infringed upon a) in defence of any person from unlawful violence; b) to effect a lawful arrest or to prevent the escape of a person lawfully detained; or c) in action lawfully taken for the purpose of quelling a riot or insurrection. It follows that if the coroner finds that there is threat to the applicant's Article 2 rights, they will not have legal footing to nevertheless allow the infringement simply to ensure that proceedings are held in public.

Articles 8 and 10 may both be restricted in wide sets of circumstances. In effect, the court will often perform a balancing exercise between these two competing sets of rights.

In making, or resisting, an application for anonymity it is therefore most useful to consider the relevant caselaw.

Relevant Cases

R (On the application of Hicks) v Inner North London Senior Coroner [2016] EWHC 1726 (Admin)

The claimants were relatives of the deceased, who had died in a road traffic collision after being pursued by police officers. From shortly after the deceased's death, hostility towards the officers began to be expressed in graphic terms on social media. This included threats to kill them. Much of the social media traffic included the father and sister of the deceased, although neither of them issued direct threats.

Having taken into account a risk assessment, the coroner granted an application under Rule 18 of the 2013 Inquests Rules. However, there was no courtroom with screening facilities. At the time the coroner made the order, she accepted that they would be seen by those in court, but effectively granted anonymity in relation to those not in the court.

When the coroner was shown the social media material, of which she had previously been unaware, she directed that the claimants, the press and the public should be excluded from the courtroom when the officers gave evidence. She arranged for them to hear the evidence from another room via audio link.

The claimants challenged this decision, relying upon the investigative obligation in Article 2 of the ECHR and the principle of open justice as supported by Article 10 of the ECHR. They argued that their right to effective participation meant that they should be present during the oral evidence of such crucial witnesses, and that there was insufficient justification for interfering with the openness of the inquest.

The application was refused. The Court found that there was nothing irrational or unfair in the coroner's finding that there was a real risk of a threat to the safety of the officers arising from third parties if the claimants learned the identity of the officers. Her decision to prevent the officers from being seen and potentially identified was correct. However, the Court added at paragraphs 41 to 43, in relation to the inherent desire not to exclude family members from the hearing room:

> "*41. As the parties are aware, the Coroner had wished to make arrangements more favourable to the family than had apparently proved possible. She had sought a hearing room which would enable the family (and the public) to be present with the four witnesses screened. I fully recognise that the closest possible participation by family members consistent with the protection of witnesses is desirable. It is helpful if family members can gain the most immediate impression of the proceedings, can hear the witnesses live and can readily consult with their legal team. It is highly undesirable to exclude family members from the hearing room, and should not be done unless it is absolutely necessary.*
>
> *42. It was with such considerations in mind that during short adjournments, this Court was able to see that arrangements were made for the relevant parts of the Inquest to take place in the Royal Courts of Justice, with family members present. This was the kind of arrangement the Coroner had wished for all along. In my view her instinct was entirely right. Once these arrangements were made, the other issues fell away.*
>
> *43. It was for these reasons that I considered the Claimants should have permission to apply for judicial review, but that the application for judicial review should be dismissed.*"

<u>R v Bedfordshire Coroner ex p Local Sunday Newspapers Ltd (2000) 164 JP 283</u>

A man was shot dead by a member of the armed response group of the Bedfordshire police force. At the inquest the coroner considered a request from the assistant chief constable in relation to the officers involved in the incident.

The request was made on the basis that members of the deceased's family held one of the officers ('Officer B') responsible for his death. Although no threats had been made to the Officer B, the coroner decided to grant the order. That decision was challenged by way of judicial review.

In dismissing the application the Court held that in order to justify anonymity the facts of the case would need to establish fear for personal or family safety. The coroner was not irrational to take into account Officer B's previous experiences in this case. He was also entitled to conclude that there was a need for special care and a risk of injury and danger to Officer B in disclosing to the criminal fraternity that he was a member of the armed response group, nor was that in the public interest. The existence of those grounds enabled the coroner to conclude that there was sufficient reason for anonymity. At 185:

> "*185. Once a reason for anonymity is established … on an objective basis, albeit of course always on the basis of a reasonable chance or a serious possibility as opposed to being in some way proof on the balance of probabilities, then a balancing act should still be performed …*
>
> *In the balancing act the following factors, of course among others, may be relevant; I indicate only those factors for the moment which are common ground:*
>
> *(a) Whether the effect is to be that the entire hearing is to be held in secret; or that only part of it is to be held in secret; or whether some of the evidence is not to be heard in public or not to be reported; or, at the end of the scale, whether, although the hearing is otherwise open and the evidence is otherwise given in public, the name or names, whether of a participant in the proceedings or of a victim or of a witness or merely of someone referred to in the course of evidence, is not to be published. The least interference in the public exercise of justice that can be tolerated is the most preferable on the one hand; but, on the other hand, if, as here, it is the least interference which is proposed then it may be easier to pass the test to achieve it.*

(b) The nature of the hearing must be relevant. It is likely to be more difficult for there to be such restrictions imposed in a criminal trial, where, for example, an accused's lawyers may or will need as much information as they can about a witness in order to be able to challenge credibility, than in an inquest or inquiry where, as here, the Coroner in any event knew the identity of the witnesses ..."

<u>R v Lord Saville of Newdigate ex p B (Bloody Sunday Inquiry) (2000) 1 WLR 1855</u>

In 1972, the inquiry into the 'Bloody Sunday' shootings granted anonymity to individual soldiers involved. The inquiry in 2000 withdrew that anonymity. The soldiers successfully challenged this decision by way of judicial review. The tribunal appealed, contending that whilst a genuine threat of reprisals remained, the need to conduct a fully open inquiry outweighed the risks involved in identifying the soldiers.

Dismissing the appeal, the Court of Appeal held that the tribunal had failed to appreciate that by conducting a painstaking inquiry spanning every issue, it was performing its judicial function correctly and also establishing public confidence in the outcome. The legislation governing the conduct of the tribunal itself contemplated that there might be parts of the evidence from which the public were excluded.

The public nature of the inquiry would be preserved despite the maintenance of anonymity. Evidence would be taken in public and reports of the proceedings published. The tribunal was clearly concerned with the views of the victims' relatives as to procedural fairness, but had neglected to give sufficient weight to the opposing views on fairness if anonymity was withdrawn. Once it became apparent that the fear of reprisal was reasonable, the fundamental question to ask was whether there was any compelling justification for the withdrawal of anonymity that had been afforded to the soldiers for the previous 27 years. The individual right to life was a fundamental freedom to which the tribunal had possibly paid insufficient attention. At paragraph 37:

> "*37. What is important to note is that when a fundamental right such as the right to life is engaged, the options available to the reasonable decision maker are curtailed. They are curtailed because it is unreasonable to reach a decision which contravenes or could contravene human rights unless there are sufficiently significant countervailing considerations. In other words it is not open to the decision maker to risk interfering with fundamental rights in the absence of compelling justification. Even the broadest discretion is constrained by the need for there to be countervailing circumstances justifying interference with human rights.*"

<u>R(A) v HM Coroner for Inner North London (2004) The Times 12 July</u>

A decision not to impose anonymity was overturned where the evidence as a whole indicated a clear objective justification for the applicants' fears for their life

<u>Re Officer L (2007) UKHL 36</u>

The appellant was the Robert Hamill Inquiry. It had refused applications by police officers for anonymity, which had been made on the basis that if they were identified they would become targets for terrorist attack. The officers successfully challenged this decision; subsequent appeals by the Inquiry led to the case coming before the House of Lords.

In allowing the Inquiry's appeal, the House of Lords stated at paragraphs 25 to 26:

> "*25. The tribunal accordingly approached the matter properly under article 2 in seeking to ascertain whether giving evidence would give rise to a materially increased risk to life. Having found that it did not, it did not require then to go on to consider whether such an increased risk, if found to exist, would come up to the threshold required of a real and immediate risk to life.*

> *26. It was also correct in asking the same question when considering the common law duty. If the risk has not been increased, then it is not unfair on that account to require a witness to give evidence. It went on, again correctly in my opinion, to assess the relevant factors other than actual risk to life which could make it unfair to require witnesses to testify without anonymity, that is, the subjective fears which many of them expressed. It carried out a proper balancing exercise and concluded that the balance came down against allowing the applications for anonymity, then took into account medical evidence in order to determine if that affected its conclusions. In my opinion the tribunal applied the correct tests and the decisions of Morgan J and the Court of Appeal cannot be sustained."*

And at paragraph 29:

> *"29. … I suggest that the exercise to be carried out by the tribunal faced with a request for anonymity should be the application of the common law test, with an excursion, if the facts require it, into the territory of article 2 . Such an excursion would only be necessary if the tribunal found that, viewed objectively, a risk to the witness's life would be created or materially increased if they gave evidence without anonymity. If so, it should decide whether that increased risk would amount to a real and immediate risk to life. If it would, then the tribunal would ordinarily have little difficulty in determining that it would be reasonable in all the circumstances to give the witnesses a degree of anonymity. That would then conclude the exercise, for that anonymity would be required by article 2 and it would be unnecessary for the tribunal to give further consideration to the matter. If there would not be a real and immediate threat to the witness's life, then article 2 would drop out of consideration and the tribunal would continue to decide the matter as one governed by the common law principles. In coming to that decision the existence of subjective fears can be taken into account, on the basis which I earlier discussed (see paragraph 22). For the same reasons as those which I have set out in paragraph 20, however, I would not regard it as essential in every case*

to commence consideration of the issue by seeking to identify such subjective fears."

PRACTICALITIES

Practicalities that may be discussed at the pre-inquest review are:

- Suitable date for the final inquest hearing;
- The venue;
- The length of the inquest;
- The timetabling of witnesses;
- Whether certain legal representatives will attend in person or by video-link;

This list is not exhaustive; it will depend on the circumstances and needs of the particular case.

WILL THERE BE COUNSEL TO THE INQUEST?

One of the questions that may arise is whether there is requirement for Counsel to the Inquest to be appointed. Counsel to the inquest will by no means be appointed in every instance. They will be reserved for those inquests which are more complex and in which the coroner would benefit from the use of assistance.

Chief Coroners Guidance No.40 *Counsel and Solicitors to the Inquest* explains as follows:

> "*1. In judge-led inquests or those where a judge has been appointed as an assistant coroner, it is usual for a legal team to be appointed including Counsel to the Inquest (CTI) and often a solicitor to the inquest. In such cases, which often involve lengthy and complex*

hearings, the team of counsel and solicitors will usually be chosen by the judge.

2. This Guidance is not concerned with such inquests being heard by judges, in which the make-up of the legal team will be a matter for the judge concerned. It is to assist a coroner (whether senior, area or assistant) in dealing with inquests that, by their very nature, may require the instruction of a barrister or solicitor to act as CTI and/or the instruction of a firm of solicitors to act at the coroner's direction.

[...]

4. The use of CTI by coroners is well-established and is analogous to the role of counsel to a public inquiry. Similarly, the use of a firm of solicitors to assist a coroner is well-established. In R v Secretary of State for Northern Ireland, Ex Parte Devine and Breslin [1998] 14 NIQB 10, Carswell J accepted that it had been proper for CTI to have been appointed and to have led questioning of witnesses. In R (Plymouth CC) v HM Coroner for Devon [2005] 1 Inquest LR at [10], Wilson J commented approvingly on the instruction of CTI."

Paragraph 5 of Guidance No.40 indicates that inquests with the following features may justify the instruction of Counsel to the Inquest and/or the use of Solicitors to the Inquest:

- Complexity;
- Novel points of law;
- Multiple IPs with legal representation;
- Large numbers of witnesses;
- Disputed/complex expert evidence and factual issues;
- Voluminous and/or complex documentation;

- National security concerns, materials covered by RIPA 2000/RIPA 2016 and other sensitive materials giving rise to special difficulties (police firearms operations, terrorism, foreign cases);

- Letters of request for evidence from jurisdictions outside the UK;

- Special measures for vulnerable witnesses;

- Adversarial subtext;

- Lengthy or very complex jury inquests;

- Long duration of the inquest; and

- A mass fatality incident involving Disaster Victim Identification (DVI) processes.

This list is non-exhaustive but gives a clear idea of the types of inquest which would justify Counsel or Solicitors to the Inquest.

Ultimately the choice of whether to instruct Counsel or Solicitors to the Inquest is a matter for the coroner (paragraph 9 of Guidance No.40). If they are instructed, the responsibility for the investigation and the inquest ultimately remains that of the coroner. The coroner marshals the evidence, lists the hearing and deals personally with all associated matters in readiness for the inquest (paragraph 14 of Guidance No.40). A coroner can instruct Counsel to the Inquest, though, to provide assistance and to examine witnesses on their behalf, so long as the coroner retains overall control of proceedings and makes judicial decisions (paragraph 15 of Guidance No.40).

In a complex or large inquest, there may be several benefits to instructing Counsel or Solicitors to the Inquest (see paragraphs 16 and 17 of Guidance No.40):

- Counsel to the inquest can talk to other counsel to narrow the issues, reduce the number of documents or witnesses and therefore reduce the length of the inquest as a whole. These informal discussions between advocates are ones which the coroner cannot hold directly;

- Work pressure on the coroner's officer and the coroner's administrative staff;

- Counsel or Solicitors to the Inquest can assist with the securing and marshalling evidence, and then disclosure of the evidence;

- Counsel and Solicitors to the inquest can assist with the management of pre-inquest review hearings;

- Overall, Counsels or Solicitors to the Inquest can allow the investigation and inquest to proceed as expeditiously as possible.

Some examples of tasks which may be undertaken by Counsel or Solicitors to the Inquest are (see paragraph 7 of Guidance No.40):

- Provide advice or submissions on specific points (e.g. to draft submissions on difficult points of law);

- Assist more generally in preparing for and conducting the inquest hearing on behalf of the coroner;

- Assist with particular tasks such as review of documents, preparation of material for disclosure or correspondence;

- Counsel may be used in a junior support role for some cases where that junior counsel has supported the coroner in managing the documents, disclosure, liaison with other counsel and taking a detailed and accurate note of key parts of the evidence to feed into later witnesses' questions.

There are, though, some important limits to the powers of Counsel and Solicitors to the Inquest:

- Where the Counsel to the Inquest provides guidance to the coroner on potentially contentious issues of law or on significant and potentially contentious points of procedure, that guidance should be given in open court;

- There are some functions the coroner cannot ask the Counsel to the Inquest to perform (e.g. directing the jury as to law and summing up the evidence);

- Submissions made by the Counsel to the Inquest are made from an independent viewpoint so should reflect their honest view of the correct legal position rather than 'instructions' given by the coroner;

- Any rulings of the coroner must represent the coroner's own judicial decision. The coroner must always exercise independent judgment and take responsibility for all rulings.

CHAPTER SIX

SCOPE

THE TWO TYPES OF INQUEST

One of the most important decisions for a coroner can be the scope of the inquest – i.e. will the inquest be a traditional 'Jamieson' style inquest, or will it be an Article 2 inquest?

This section falls within the 'pre-inquest' section of the book. However, bear in mind that the coroner may well decide to adjourn final consideration of scope of the inquest until the evidence has been heard. In cases where the answer is not immediately clear, this may be a sensible approach: for example, as the evidence comes out it may become clear that a public body could be responsible for systemic failures which led to the death.

In broad terms, the two types of inquest are as follows:

1. A *Jamieson* inquest. This is also known as a 'traditional' inquest. In a *Jamieson* inquest, the question of 'how' a person died is interpreted as 'by what means'. The inquest will not explore the wider circumstances behind a person's death except insofar as that directly relates to 'by what means' the person died. For example, circumstances leading to a deterioration in a person's mental state might be relevant to the coroner's ultimate conclusion that a person died by suicide (such as in the recent case of *Dove v HM Assistant Coroner for Teeside and Hartlepool* [2023] EWCA Civ 289);

2. A *Middleton* inquest. This is also known as an 'Article 2' inquest. In a *Middleton* inquest, the question of 'how' a person died is interpreted far more broadly as 'by what means and in what

circumstances'. The inquest will accordingly consider the broader relevant circumstances behind a person's death, including systemic issues. For example, in a case where a person is said to have committed suicide in custody, an Article 2 inquest is likely to explore the systems in place within the prison to prevent self-harm and suicide.

For many years, the *Jamieson* model was the blueprint for the structure and aims of a modern inquest. It is for this reason that it is also sometimes called a 'traditional' inquest. The advent of the Human Rights Act 1998 and, most importantly, the case of *R(Middleton) v West Somerset Coroner* (2004) UKHL 10 shone a light on the need to ensure that inquests took account of the State's responsibility both to protect life and to adequately investigate potential breaches of the protection of life.

The *Middleton* inquest is now enshrined in section 5(2) of the 2009 Act:

"***5 Matters to be ascertained***

(1) The purpose of an investigation under this Part into a person's death is to ascertain—

(a) who the deceased was;

(b) how, when and where the deceased came by his or her death;

(c) the particulars (if any) required by the 1953 Act to be registered concerning the death.

(2) Where necessary in order to avoid a breach of any Convention rights (within the meaning of the Human Rights Act 1998 (c. 42)), the purpose mentioned in subsection (1)(b) is to be read as including the purpose of ascertaining in what circumstances the deceased came by his or her death."

In determining which type of inquest is most appropriate, the coroner will therefore consider the following question: is it arguable that the UK has breached its substantive obligation to protect the right to life because it owed a duty to the deceased? The UK will have owed a duty to the deceased where the person has died whilst in custody of the state (such as a prisoner in police custody), or at the hands of state agents (such as whilst being arrested by police).

a) If the answer is 'yes', then the coroner will hold an Article 2 inquest;

b) If the answer is 'no', then the coroner will hold a *Jamieson* inquest;

c) If the answer is more ambiguous (for example, there may be arguments as to whether certain types of State care amount to being 'in custody of the State') the coroner will need to listen to competing arguments, consider precedent and may well adjourn their consideration of the issue until more is known about the evidence.

The decision will depend to a large extent on the features of that particular case. There is, though, a large body of caselaw which provides useful guidance in determining the scope of your particular inquest. A selection of those decisions which the author considers most helpful are set out below. Just before turning to those cases, though, it is first important to understand Article 2 of the European Convention on Human Rights, which now forms the backbone to inquest proceedings in general and *Middleton* inquests in particular.

ARTICLE 2 OF THE EUROPEAN CONVENTION ON HUMAN RIGHTS

Article 2 of the European Convention on Human Rights ("ECHR") provides:

> "*1. Everyone's right to life shall be protected by law. No one shall be deprived of his life intentionally save in the execution of a sentence of*

a court following his conviction of a crime for which this penalty is provided by law.

2. Deprivation of life shall not be regarded as inflicted in contravention of this article when it results from the use of force which is no more than absolutely necessary:

(a) in defence of any person from unlawful violence;

(b) in order to effect a lawful arrest or to prevent the escape of a person lawfully detained;

(c) in action lawfully taken for the purpose of quelling a riot or insurrection."

Article 2 of the ECHR can be divided into three broad obligations:

1. The positive obligation – the duty to take appropriate steps to protect life. (This is broken down further into two components: (1) the general or systemic duty; and (2) the operational duty.)

2. The negative obligation – the prohibition of intentional and unlawful taking of life by state agents (this is also broken down into a general / systemic duty and an operational duty);

3. The procedural obligation – the duty to investigate potential violations of the negative or positive obligations.

Under the substantive obligations, the State is not only bound not to take life without justification but also to establish a framework of laws, precautions, procedures and means of enforcement which will – to the greatest extent reasonably practicable – protect life.

RELEVANT CASES (ARTICLE 2 OF THE ECHR)

Osman v United Kingdom (2000) 29 EHRR 245

This is a leading case on the application of Article 2. In this case the European Court of Human Rights (ECtHR) set out the positive obligations under Article 2 and emphasised the high threshold for establishing a breach of the State's duties.

Osman, a teenage boy, was seriously injured and his father was killed after being shot by Osman's former teacher, who had become obsessed by the teenager. Before the shooting there had been a number of concerning incidents against Osman, including damage to his home. Osman and his mother brought a civil action for negligence against the police but this was ultimately struck out by the Court of Appeal. They then applied to the ECtHR, contending that the State had failed to protect the lives of Osman and his father, and failed to protect the family from harassment. They argued that this breached their rights under Articles 2 and 8, and that they had been denied access to a court in respect of those breaches, contrary to Article 6(1) of the ECHR.

The ECtHR held that there had been no violation of Art.2 (its decision in relation to the other claims is not set out here, as not relevant for our purposes). The ECtHR held that the State was not in breach of its positive obligation to take preventative measures to protect an individual whose life was at risk from another. There was a requirement that the police knew or ought to have known that there was a real and immediate threat to Osman and his father's lives from the perpetrator. This was not met as none of the incidents prior to the shootings were life-threatening, there was no proof that the killer was responsible for those acts and there was no evidence that he was mentally ill or prone to violence;

In the course of this discussion, the Court outlined the general obligations under A2 that a State is expected to uphold:

> "*2. As to the alleged failure of the authorities to protect the rights to life of Ali and Ahmet Osman*

115. The Court notes that the first sentence of Article 2(1) enjoins the State not only to refrain from the intentional and unlawful taking of life, but also to take appropriate steps to safeguard the lives of those within its jurisdiction. It is common ground that the State's obligation in this respect extends beyond its primary duty to secure the right to life by putting in place effective criminal law provisions to deter the commission of offences against the person backed up by law-enforcement machinery for the prevention, suppression and sanctioning of breaches of such provisions. It is thus accepted by those appearing before the Court that Article 2 of the Convention may also imply in certain well-defined circumstances a positive obligation on the authorities to take preventive operational measures to protect an individual whose life is at risk from the criminal acts of another individual. The scope of this obligation is a matter of dispute between the parties.

116. For the Court, and bearing in mind the difficulties involved in policing modern societies, the unpredictability of human conduct and the operational choices which must be made in terms of priorities and resources, such an obligation must be interpreted in a way which does not impose an impossible or disproportionate burden on the authorities. Accordingly, not every claimed risk to life can entail for the authorities a Convention requirement to take operational measures to prevent that risk from materializing. Another relevant consideration is the need to ensure that the police exercise their powers to control and prevent crime in a manner which fully respects the due process and other guarantees which legitimately place restraints on the scope of their action to investigate crime and bring offenders to justice, including the guarantees contained in Articles 5 and 8 of the Convention.

In the opinion of the Court where there is an allegation that the authorities have violated their positive obligation to protect the right to life in the context of their above-mentioned duty to prevent and suppress offences against the person, it must be established to its satisfaction that the authorities knew or ought to have known at the time of the existence of a real and immediate risk to the life of an identified individual or individuals from the criminal acts of a third party and that they failed to take measures within the scope of their powers which, judged reasonably, might have been expected to avoid that risk. The Court does not accept the Government's view that the failure to perceive the risk to life in the circumstances known at the time or to take preventive measures to avoid that risk must be tantamount to gross negligence or wilful disregard of the duty to protect life. Such a rigid standard must be considered to be incompatible with the requirements of Article 1 of the Convention and the obligations of Contracting States under that Article to secure the practical and effective protection of the rights and freedoms laid down therein, including Article 2. For the Court, and having regard to the nature of the right protected by Article 2, a right fundamental in the scheme of the Convention, it is sufficient for an applicant to show that the authorities did not do all that could be reasonably expected of them to avoid a real and immediate risk to life of which they have or ought to have knowledge. This is a question which can only be answered in the light of all the circumstances of any particular case."

The operational duty outlined in this case is now known as the *Osman* test. The test has now been repeated in numerous cases since *Osman* both by the domestic courts and the EctHR.

<u>Oneryildiz v Turkey (2005) 41 EHRR 20</u>

In this case the ECtHR set out guidance as to the ambit of Article 2. At paragraph 71:

"71. … the Court reiterates that Art.2 does not solely concern deaths resulting from the use of force by agents of the state but also, in the first sentence of its first paragraph, lays down a positive obligation on states to take appropriate steps to safeguard the lives of those within their jurisdiction.

The Court considers that this obligation must be construed as applying in the context of any activity, whether public or not, in which the right to life may be at stake, and a fortiori in the case of industrial activities, which by their very nature are dangerous, such as the operation of waste-collection sites ..."

And at paragraph 89:

"*89. The positive obligation to take all appropriate steps to safeguard life for the purposes of Art.2 entails above all a primary duty on the state to put in place a legislative and administrative framework designed to provide effective deterrence against threats to the right to life.*"

Mitchell v Glasgow City Council (2009) UKHL 11

The House of Lords stated as follows in relation to the operation of Article 2 at paragraph 66:

"*66. ...where a state has assumed responsibility for an individual, whether by taking him into custody, by imprisoning him, detaining him under mental health legislation, or conscripting him into the armed forces, the state assumes responsibility for that individual's safety. So in these circumstances police authorities, prison authorities, health authorities and the armed forces are all subject to positive obligations to protect the lives of those in their care. The authorities must therefore take general measures to employ and train competent staff and to adopt appropriate systems of work that will protect the lives of the people for whose welfare they have made themselves responsible. These are general obligations, not directed at any particular individual, but designed to protect all those in the authorities' care ...*

Authorities which are under these general obligations to persons in their care may also come under a distinct, additional, 'operational' obligation to take special preventive measures to protect a particular individual in their care. That operational obligation arises only where the authority knows, or ought to know, of a 'real and immediate risk' to the life of the particular individual."

<u>Rabbone v Pennine Care NHS Foundation Trust (2010) EWCA Civ 698</u>

The Court of Appeal found that Article 2 of the ECHR did not impose an operational obligation towards all persons who were at real and immediate risk of death. So health trusts did not have operational obligations under art.2 to voluntary patients who were suffering from physical or mental illness. The proper remedy for clinical negligence, even where a real and immediate risk of death had been disregarded, was an action in negligence. At paragraphs 62 to 64:

> *"62. Having reviewed the authorities and considered counsel's submissions, I have come to the conclusion that detention under the Mental Health Act makes a critical difference. It is clear that article 2 of the Convention does not impose upon the state an operational obligation towards all persons who are at "real and immediate risk" of death. For example, state officials are not obliged to stop those with suicidal intent from travelling to Switzerland: see Lord Scott in Savage's case, at para 10. In addition to the "real and immediate risk" of death, there must be some additional element before state authorities come under the operational obligation. Examples of the additional element are (a) involvement of the police with a criminal who is liable to kill the individual concerned or (b) the fact that the individual concerned is detained by the state.*
>
> *63. On the law as it stands, I do not believe that health trusts have the article 2 operational obligation to voluntary patients in hospital, who are suffering from physical or mental illness, even where there is a "real and immediate" risk of death. In my view it is not possible to separate such patients into categories and to say that the operational obligation is owed to some categories of voluntary patients, but not others. A patient undergoing major heart surgery may be at just as great a risk of death as a schizophrenic patient with suicidal ideation.*
>
> *64. It is important for court users (patients, NHS trusts, legal advisers and others) that legal obligations and liabilities should be clearly*

defined and understood. I do not believe that it either is or should be the law that voluntary patients fall into different categories, some of whom (or some of whose families) can claim under article 2 but others of whom cannot. The remedy for clinical negligence, even where a "real and immediate" risk of death has been disregarded, is an action in negligence".

RELEVANT CASES (JAMIESON INQUESTS)

R v North Humberside Coroner ex p Jamieson (1995) QB 1

This case is one of the key authorities on the scope of an inquest; an entire subset of inquests are named 'Jamieson inquests'.

Michael Jamieson was a prisoner who was also a known suicide risk. Despite the fact that he was known to be high-risk of self-harm, he was left alone at night in a single cell without supervision. One night he tragically hung himself in his cell.

At the inquest into his death, the coroner directed the jury that whilst they could return a verdict of suicide, they could not go further and return a verdict of suicide contributed to by lack of care (now known as 'neglect').

Mr Jamieson's brother, Roy Jamieson, judicially reviewed the Coroner's decision not to leave the wider verdict to the jury.

The Divisional Court dismissed the application. A subsequent appeal to the Court of Appeal was dismissed as well.

During the course of the judicial discussion, Sir Thomas Bingham reviewed the relevant case law and legislation. He recorded 14 general conclusions. The key ones for our purposes, and indeed the ones that meant that this case leant its name to a certain type of inquest, are the conclusions as to the role and scope of an inquest:

"(1) *An inquest is a fact-finding inquiry conducted by a coroner, with or without a jury, to establish reliable answers to four important but limited factual questions. The first of these relates to the identity of the deceased, the second to the place of his death, the third to the time of death. In most cases these questions are not hard to answer but in a minority of cases the answer may be problematical. The fourth question, and that to which evidence and inquiry are most often and most closely directed, relates to how the deceased came by his death. Rule 36 requires that the proceedings and evidence shall be directed solely to ascertaining these matters and forbids any expression of opinion on any other matter.*

(2) *Both in section 11(5)(b)(ii) of the Act of 1988 and in rule 36(1)(b) of the Rules of 1984, "how" is to be understood as meaning "by what means." It is noteworthy that the task is not to ascertain how the deceased died, which might raise general and far-reaching issues, but "how . . . the deceased came by his death," a more limited question directed to the means by which the deceased came by his death.*

(3) *It is not the function of a coroner or his jury to determine, or appear to determine, any question of criminal or civil liability, to apportion guilt or attribute blame. This principle is expressed in rule 42 of the Rules of 1984. The rule does, however, treat criminal and civil liability differently: whereas a verdict must not be framed so as to appear to determine any question of criminal liability on the part of a named person , thereby legitimating a verdict of unlawful killing provided no one is named, the prohibition on returning a verdict so as to appear to determine any question of civil liability is unqualified, applying whether anyone is named or not.*

(4) *This prohibition in the Rules is fortified by considerations of fairness. Our law accords a defendant accused of crime or a party alleged to have committed a civil wrong certain safeguards rightly regarded as essential to the fairness of the proceedings, among them a clear statement in writing of the alleged wrongdoing, a right to call any relevant and admissible evidence and a right to address factual*

submissions to the tribunal of fact. These rights are not granted, and the last is expressly denied by the Rules, to a party whose conduct may be impugned by evidence given at an inquest.

(5) *It may be accepted that in case of conflict the statutory duty to ascertain how the deceased came by his death must prevail over the prohibition in rule 42. But the scope for conflict is small. Rule 42 applies, and applies only, to the verdict. Plainly the coroner and the jury may explore facts bearing on criminal and civil liability. But the verdict may not appear to determine any question of criminal liability on the part of a named person nor any question of civil liability.*

(6) *There can be no objection to a verdict which incorporates a brief, neutral, factual statement: "the deceased was drowned when his sailing dinghy capsized in heavy seas," "the deceased was killed when his car was run down by an express train on a level crossing," "the deceased died from crush injuries sustained when gates were opened at Hillsborough Stadium." But such verdict must be factual, expressing no judgment or opinion, and it is not the jury's function to prepare detailed factual statements.*"

<u>R v Sussex Western District Coroner ex p Homberg (1994) 158 JP 357</u>

Following a fire in which five people died an inquest was held. The coroner indicated his dissatisfaction with those representing two families and refused to call a witness whose evidence they wished to adduce. After this refusal the two families and their legal representatives withdrew from the inquest and lodged an application for judicial review, alleging several improprieties in the case. One of the improprieties was that a defective direction had been given as to the verdict of unlawful killing.

The application for judicial review was refused. In the circumstances the jury could not, on the evidence have reached any other verdict, despite the inadequate direction. In the course of the judicial discussion Simon Brown LJ said the following as to the coroner's duty to inquire 'how' the deceased came by their death:

> *"It is clear that the coroner's over-riding duty is to inquire 'how' the deceased came by his death and that duty prevails over any inhibition against appearing to determine questions of criminal or civil liability . . Secondly, the cases establish that although the is word 'how' is to be widely interpreted, it means 'by what means' rather than 'in what broad circumstances' . In short the inquiry must focus on matters directly causative of death and must indeed, be confined to these matters alone (save for ascertainment of the other specific details mentioned in r36(1)). The recent, 11th edition of Jervis on Coroners puts it like this: 'The question of how the deceased came by his death is of course wider than merely finding the principal cause of death, and it is therefore right and proper that the coroner should inquire into acts and omissions which are directly responsible for the death.' and 'The duty to inquire 'how' the deceased dies does not to my mind properly encompass inquiry also into the underlying responsibility for every circumstance which may be said to have contributed to the death."*

<u>R (Worthington) v Cumbria Coroner (2018) EWHC 3386</u>

The claimant applied for an order to remove references to sexual abuse from a coroner's report. The evidence indicated that the claimant had perpetrated a penetrative anal assault on his very young daughter in the hours before her death. The claimant did not challenge the coroner's factual findings, but claimed that he had erred in including the reference to anal penetration in the section of his review entitled 'Conclusion as to Death' and in his Record of Inquest.

The claimant submitted that, once the coroner had concluded at the findings of fact stage that anal penetration was not causative of death, that penetration passed beyond the means of death into the wider surrounding circumstances and could not lawfully be included in the determination of 'how' the young girl came by her death.

In dismissing the application, the Court held that the coroner had not erred in recording his finding of anal penetration in his determination. The reference did not compromise s.5(3) because it did not express an opinion, but merely repeated a finding of fact made earlier in the review. Nor did the reference stray beyond the means by which P came by her death into the wider circumstances surrounding that death.

The coroner had correctly characterised the fact of anal penetration as an integral part of the factual matrix which formed the immediate circumstances of the child's death. It was essential to explain why P was in the unsafe sleeping environment which had caused her death. It was also clearly necessary for the coroner to explain in his review why he had concluded that the death was not an unlawful killing or accidental death.

At paragraph 51:

> "*...it would be wrong as a matter of principle for this court to attempt to micromanage inquests by constraining the proper discretion of a Coroner to record the answer to the "how" question in light of all his findings of fact. A court should be cautious before interfering to require the striking out of unchallengeable findings of fact which a coroner has carefully considered to be sufficiently important by way of explanation of the means of death to include them within a determination of a section 5(1) question including how an individual came by his or her death.*"

<u>R (Takoushis) v Inner North London Coroner (2005) EWCA Civ 1440</u>

The deceased had a history of serious mental health problems. He was seen by a member of the public apparently preparing to commit suicide by jumping off a bridge and was taken to hospital. The hospital's triage system required patients such as him to be seen by a doctor within 10 minutes of arrival – this didn't happen.

By the time a doctor attended to assess the deceased, he had absconded and he subsequently committed suicide.

The family requested that a jury be called at the inquest and that the inquest be adjourned so that they could obtain expert evidence. The coroner refused their application, ruling that there had been no systemic neglect and there was no defect in the triage system itself. In any event, the coroner held, the later changes to the triage system meant a breakdown of that system was less likely. The widow of the deceased appealed.

The primary question was whether the coroner had investigated the relevant issues fully, having concluded before the inquest that there was no systemic neglect on the facts, with this decision leading to narrower evidence being heard.

The Court of Appeal found that the coroner had not investigated the relevant issues fully; he could not properly conclude that there was no systemic failure on the evidence available before the inquest.

At paragraphs 48 to 49:

> "*48. It was recognised on all sides that the circumstances in which Mr Takoushis came to leave the hospital, only shortly after he had apparently taken steps to jump into the river and gone voluntarily to the hospital and only shortly before he in fact jumped into the river and thus took his own life, were by no means too remote from his death so that, in Sir Thomas Bingham MR's words, they became too remote to form a proper part of the investigation.*
>
> *49. The question is whether those circumstances were fully investigated in the way contemplated in both ex p Jamieson … and ex p Dallaglio … Such an investigation surely involved investigating both what the system at the hospital was and how it operated on the day in question. The coroner recognised that but, in our judgment, did not investigate the system in sufficient detail …*"

And at paragraphs 105 to 106:

> "*105. It seems to us that … where a person dies as a result of what is arguably medical negligence in an NHS hospital, the state must have a system which provides for the practical and effective investigation of*

the facts and for the determination of civil liability. Unlike in the cases of death in custody, the system does not have to provide for an investigation initiated by the state but may include such an investigation. Thus the question in each case is whether the system as a whole, including both any investigation initiated by the state and the possibility of civil and criminal proceedings and of a disciplinary process, satisfies the requirements of article 2 as identified by the European court … namely (as just stated) the practical and effective investigation of the facts and the determination of civil liability.

106. The question is whether the system in operation in England in this case meets those requirements. In our opinion it does … in the context of the other procedures available, an inquest of the traditional kind, without any reading down of the 1988 Act by giving a wider meaning to 'how' as envisaged in [Middleton], and provided that it carries out the kind of full and fair investigation which is discussed earlier in this judgment and which (we hope) will now take place, in our opinion satisfies the requirement that there will be a public investigation of the facts which will be both practical and effective. Moreover, the family will be able to take a full part."

R (on the application of Leeson) v HM Coroner for Manchester South [2023] EWHC 62 (Admin)

The applicant was the father of the deceased, a woman who had died in a holiday home swimming pool while on holiday with her husband. The medical evidence showed that she had drowned but she also had injuries consistent with either unlawful force being applied to cause her to drown, or consistent with attempts at rescue and resuscitation by the husband.

The inquest started but was adjourned whilst the husband was prosecuted for murder. As part of the criminal case the prosecution adduced evidence that he had taken out excessive life and travel insurance policies on the life of the deceased. In the event, the Judge in the criminal case stopped those proceedings as he found there was no case to answer (i.e. there was insufficient evidence upon which a jury properly directed could properly convict).

Accordingly, the inquest was resumed. The coroner included evidence as to the deceased's health and medical history but determined that the inquest would not include any evidence from events occurring before her arrival on holiday or after her death. Consequently, the husband's taking out of the life insurance policies and much of the evidence concerning his finances, alleged lies and actions after the deceased's death would not be heard.

The applicant successfully challenged this decision by the coroner by way of judicial review. In granting the application, the Court held (paragraphs 25 to 34):

> *"25. There was no material dispute between the claimant and first interested party as to the relevant principles of law relating to this claim. First the Coroners Court is a creature of statute. The relevant statute is now the CJA 2009.*
>
> *26. Secondly an inquest is not a trial. It is an inquisitorial process designed to get at the truth of how a deceased has died.*
>
> *27. Thirdly, following the judgment of the majority of the Supreme Court in R(Maughan) v HM's Senior Coroner for Oxfordshire [2020] UKSC 46; [2021] AC 454, a conclusion of unlawful killing will be determined on the civil standard of the balance of probabilities, which is the same standard which applies to all other conclusions of an inquest. The previous approach, whereby a conclusion of suicide or unlawful killing could only be returned if the Coroner (or jury) were sure of that conclusion, was held to be wrong. Evidence of motive may assist in determining whether a conclusion of unlawful killing should be returned, see R (Secretary of State for Justice) v HM Deputy Coroner for the Eastern District of West Yorkshire [2012] EWHC 1634 (Admin); [2012] Inquest LR 76 at paragraph 28.*

28. Fourthly, a Coroner must ensure that relevant facts are the subject of public scrutiny, particularly if there is evidence of foul play. This means that an inquest is not restricted to the last link in the chain of causation. However, the determination of the scope of an inquest is a matter for the discretion of the Coroner, see R v North Humberside Coroner ex parte Jamieson [1995] QB 1 at 26, R(Sreedharan) v HM Coroner for the County of Greater Manchester [2013] EWCA Civ 181; [2013] Med LR 89 at paragraph 18 , and Coroner for the Birmingham Inquests v Hambleton and others [2018] EWCA Civ 2081; [2019] 1 WLR 3417 at 32, and 46-48 .

29. Fifthly, there is a high hurdle in showing that a Coroner's decision as to scope is either unlawful or irrational, R (Sreedharan) at paragraph 48.

Impermissible restriction as to scope

30. In my judgment, the Coroner's ruling as to the temporal scope of the inquest into the death of Ms Leeson was not a lawful one. As appears above the Coroner has a statutory duty to carry out an investigation to discover the truth about how Ms Leeson came to die. It is apparent that the Coroner had this obligation in mind because he resumed the inquest after Mr McPherson's acquittal at the conclusion of the criminal proceedings. It is also right to record that it is for the Coroner to decide what evidence is to be adduced at the inquest. However the discretion about which evidence to call must be exercised on a rational basis.

31. In my judgment it was not rational to limit the evidence to be called at the inquest to the period from when Ms Leeson arrived in Denmark until the day of her death. This is because the ruling excluded evidence about matters which had occurred before Ms Leeson's arrival in Denmark, and evidence about matters which had occurred after her death, which was relevant to the issue of whether Ms Leeson had suffered an accidental death or had been unlawfully killed. The evidence was summarised by Goose J. in his ruling on the submission of no case to answer, and in particular included the evidence as to dealings with insurance policies which pre-dated Ms Leeson's arrival in Denmark.

32. This evidence of the insurance policies was relevant to the statutory issue of "how ... the deceased came by ... her death", see section 5(1)(b) of the CJA 2009 . This is because the taking out of the insurance policies on the death of Ms Leeson might (but whether it does will be for the Coroner sitting without a jury) make a conclusion of unlawful killing and not accidental death more likely in circumstances where it seems that the medical evidence might not (but again this will be for the Coroner) enable a determination to be made between accidental death or unlawful killing. This is because whether the taking out of the insurance policies provided a motive or reason for the unlawful killing of Ms Leeson can be appropriately considered when the Coroner decides the statutory question of "how" Ms Leeson came by her death. It follows that in my judgment the Coroner took an impermissibly narrow approach to the financial and circumstantial matters considered in the context of the criminal trial. The Coroner was right to note that those matters were "obviously relevant in the context of a prosecution" for murder, but they were also "obviously relevant" to the issue of whether unlawful killing or accidental death is a more likely conclusion for this inquest given the apparent state of the medical evidence.

33. I agree that Mr Browne KC was right to say that the effect of the Coroner's ruling made on 18 August 2021 did not exclude the possibility of a determination of either unlawful killing or accidental death, but the ruling did exclude relevant evidence about whether a conclusion of unlawful killing might be more likely than a conclusion of accidental death, for no proper reason. It is established that any determination at the inquest may not be framed in such a way as to appear to determine any question of criminal liability on the part of any named person, see section 10(2) of the CJA 2009, but this does not mean that the Coroner should exclude evidence relevant to the statutory question to be determined at the inquest.

> *34. Therefore in my judgment the ruling of the Coroner made on 18 August 2021 as to the scope of the inquest should be quashed. It was common ground at the hearing that it would be appropriate to remit the matter to the Coroner to revisit the ruling as to the scope of the inquest in the light of the judgments given by this Court."*

Dove v Assistant Coroner for Teeside (2023) EWCA Civ 289

The deceased was 42 when she died from an overdose. She had physical and mental health problems. The Department for Work and Pensions assessed her in 2012 as eligible for employment and support allowance (ESA) as she was functionally incapable of working.

In 2016 she fell to be reassessed and requested a home visit. The department did not deal with her request and required her to attend an assessment. She failed to attend. The department decided that she had shown no good cause for the failure and had not shown a limited capability for work. It stopped her ESA on 7 February 2017. She died exactly two weeks later, on 21 February 2017.

The mother believed that the ESA situation had caused the deceased extra stress and contributed to her death. The coroner stated that it was outside her remit, when conducting a *Jamieson* inquest, to question the department's decisions and recorded suicide as the cause of death.

After the inquest, an independent case examiner (ICE) investigated the department's handling of the case. Her report found significant failings on the part of the department. An expert psychiatrist's report concluded that it was likely that the deceased's mental state at the time of her death would have been substantially affected by the decision to withdraw her ESA.

The deceased's mother made application under section 13 of the Coroners Act 1988 for a fresh inquest (see chapter 15 for discussion of this type of application). The Divisional Court, though, held that the fresh evidence in the reports did not mean there should be a fresh inquest.

The mother appealed against that decision. She argued that either a fresh *Jamieson* inquest to determine the circumstances of the deceased's death was required, or that the state's investigative obligation under ECHR art.2 was engaged and a fresh inquest was required on that basis.

The appeal was allowed in part – the fresh *Jamieson* inquest was ordered, but the Court held that Article 2 of the ECHR was not engaged.

In allowing the appeal, the Court found that the psychiatrist's report provided expert evidence about the way in which the cessation of benefits was likely to have affected the deceased's state of mind. That was well within the scope of a *Jamieson* inquest. It went to the issue of intention, which was an element which had to be established before a conclusion of suicide was entered.

Further, that evidence would assist the coroner in deciding whether to enter a narrative conclusion to reflect the extreme anxiety and distress that the deceased might have been suffering. It would be open to a coroner with the benefit of the report to find that the sudden withdrawal of benefits had contributed to the deterioration in the deceased's mental health, and to include reference to that fact within the conclusions part of the record of inquest.

In relation to the claim that Article 2 was engaged, the Court held that the evidence did not establish that the department had owed the deceased an Article 2 operational duty. The operational duty applied in some circumstances to require the State to take positive steps to protect life, including the prevention of a real and immediate risk to life, which included a risk of suicide. It had not been established that there had been a real and immediate risk of which the State had had knowledge.

RELEVANT CASES (MIDDLETON / ARTICLE 2 INQUESTS)

R (Middleton) v West Somerset Coroner (2004) UKHL 10

This is a landmark case in terms of the scope of inquests, and lends its name to 'Article 2' inquests. This case found that the inquest regime of the time, as it stood under *Jamieson*, did not always satisfy the United Kingdom's duties under Article 2 of the ECHR.

An inquest was held into the death of a prisoner who had hung himself in prison. There was evidence that he was depressed and receiving medication at the time of his death. The jury returned a verdict (as it was then called; it is now called a conclusion) that the deceased had killed himself while the balance of his mind was disturbed. However, they also handed the coroner a note containing factual conclusions which indicated that they considered the prison service to have failed in its duty of care to the deceased.

The coroner had directed the jury that their findings were confined to the identity of the deceased and to how, when and where he came by his death. The coroner accordingly directed them that they could express no opinion on any other matter – and that since they were prohibited from framing a verdict in such a way as to appear to determine questions of criminal liability on the part of a named person, or civil liability, they could not return a verdict of neglect.

The coroner therefore refused the family's request to append the note to the inquisition. The deceased's mother challenged the coroner's direction to the jury and the decision not to publish the note by way of judicial review.

The first instance judge made a declaration that there was a breach of the State's Article 2 procedural investigative duty by virtue of the restrictions on the verdict. The Secretary of State for the Home Department (who was an interested party) appealed to the Court of Appeal.

The appeal was allowed in part. The Court of Appeal found that systemic, although not individual, neglect was a finding open to the jury where the inquest was the means by which the A2 procedural duty was to be met.

The Secretary of State for the Home Department again appealed, this time to the House of Lords.

The House of Lords allowed the appeal in part and set the Court of Appeal's declaration aside. At paragraphs 30 to 37:

> *"30. In some cases the state's procedural obligation may be discharged by criminal proceedings. This is most likely to be so where a defendant pleads not guilty and the trial involves a full exploration of the facts surrounding the death. It is unlikely to be so if the defendant's plea of guilty is accepted (as in Edwards 35 EHRR 487), or the issue at trial is the mental state of the defendant (as in Amin [2003] 3 WLR 1169), because in such cases the wider issues will probably not be explored.*
>
> *31. In some other cases, short verdicts in the traditional form will enable the jury to express their conclusion on the central issue canvassed at the inquest. McCann 21 EHRR 97 has already been given as an example: see para 14 above. The same would be true if the central issue at the inquest were whether the deceased had taken his own life or been killed by another: by choosing between verdicts of suicide and unlawful killing, the jury would make clear its factual conclusion. But it is plain that in other cases a strict Ex p Jamieson [1995] QB 1 approach will not meet what has been identified above as the Convention requirement. In Keenan 33 EHRR 913 the inquest verdict of death by misadventure and the certification of asphyxiation by hanging as the cause of death did not express the jury's conclusion on the events leading up to the death. Similarly, verdicts of unlawful killing in Edwards and Amin , although plainly justified, would not have enabled the jury to express any conclusion on what would undoubtedly have been the major issue at any inquest, the procedures which led in each case to the deceased and his killer sharing a cell.*

32. The conclusion is inescapable that there are some cases in which the current regime for conducting inquests in England and Wales, as hitherto understood and followed, does not meet the requirements of the Convention. This is a conclusion rightly reached by the judge in this case (see para 44 below) and by the Court of Appeal both in the present case (see para 44 below) and in cases such as R (Davies) v Deputy Coroner for Birmingham [2003] EWCA Civ 1739 at [71].

33. Question (3). Can the current regime governing the conduct of inquests in England and Wales be revised so as to meet the requirements of the Convention, and if so, how?

*34. Counsel for the Secretary of State rightly suggested that the House should propose no greater revision of the existing regime than is necessary to secure compliance with the Convention, even if it were (contrary to his main submission) to reach the conclusion just expressed. The warning is salutary. There has recently been published "Death Certification and Investigation in England, Wales and Northern Ireland: The Report of a Fundamental Review", June 2003 (Cm 5831). Decisions have yet to be made on whether, and how, to give effect to the recommendations. Those decisions, when made, will doubtless take account of policy, administrative and financial *202 considerations which are not the concern of the House sitting judicially. It is correct that the scheme enacted by and under the authority of Parliament should be respected save to the extent that a change of interpretation (authorised by section 3 of the Human Rights Act 1998) is required to honour the international obligations of the United Kingdom expressed in the Convention.*

35. Only one change is in our opinion needed: to interpret "how" in section 11(5)(b)(ii) of the Act and rule 36 (1)(b) of the Rules in the broader sense previously rejected, namely as meaning not simply "by what means" but "by what means and in what circumstances".

36. This will not require a change of approach in some cases, where a traditional short form verdict will be quite satisfactory, but it will call for a change of approach in others: paras 30-31 above. In the latter class of case it must be for the coroner, in the exercise of his discretion, to decide how best, in the particular case, to elicit the jury's conclusion on the central issue or issues. This may be done by inviting a form of verdict expanded beyond those suggested in form 22 of Schedule 4 to the Rules. It may be done, and has (even if very rarely) been done, by inviting a narrative form of verdict in which the jury's factual conclusions are briefly summarised. It may be done by inviting the jury's answer to factual questions put by the coroner. If the coroner invites either a narrative verdict or answers to questions, he may find it helpful to direct the jury with reference to some of the matters to which a sheriff will have regard in making his determination under section 6 of the Fatal Accidents and Sudden Deaths Inquiry (Scotland) Act 1976: where and when the death took place; the cause or causes of such death; the defects in the system which contributed to the death; and any other factors which are relevant to the circumstances of the death. It would be open to parties appearing or represented at the inquest to make submissions to the coroner on the means of eliciting the jury's factual conclusions and on any questions to be put, but the choice must be that of the coroner and his decision should not be disturbed by the courts unless strong grounds are shown.

37. The prohibition in rule 36(2) of the expression of opinion on matters not comprised within sub-rule (1) must continue to be respected. But it must be read with reference to the broader interpretation of "how" in section 11(5)(b)(ii) and rule 36(1) and does not preclude conclusions of fact as opposed to expressions of opinion. However the jury's factual conclusion is conveyed, rule 42 should not be infringed. Thus there must be no finding of criminal liability on the part of a named person. Nor must the verdict appear to determine any question of civil liability."

R (Donne LePage) v HM Assistant Deputy Coroner for Inner South London (2012) EWHC 1485

The deceased had been stopped and searched by police. A wrap containing cocaine was found on her person. She was arrested and taken to a police station. However whilst in custody she collapsed and coughed up pinkish liquid. An ambulance was called and she was taken to hospital where she suffered seizures and a cardiac arrest. She died two days later. A post-mortem determined that S had died from cardio-respiratory failure and acute cocaine toxicity. An inquest was opened to consider issues including the original stop and search at the scene, the cause of death, S's care and management at the police station, and her strip-searching and restraint at the police station.

In her summing up the coroner directed the jury to return a short-form verdict of accidental death and to supplement that with a narrative. She did not leave to the jury issues of restraint, force, search or training.

The jury returned a verdict of accidental death, with a short statement of narrative stating that S coughed up a plastic bag which had contained cocaine which she had chewed and swallowed, although the jury were unable to say when, where or how that had happened.

The family applied for judicial review of the coroner's decision not to call a forensic pathologist whose reports showed that restraint and search might have caused or contributed to the deceased's death. They also applied to judicially review the coroner's decision not to call evidence of police training about custody procedures, including restraint and collapse.

In refusing the application, the Court stated at paragraphs 43 to 44:

> "*43. In my judgment the coroner had a discretion whether to call Dr James and she exercised that discretion reasonably and fairly. She did not act Wednesbury unreasonably. As the decision in R (Lewis) v Mid and North Shropshire Coroner [2010] 1 WLR 1836 shows, she had no duty to call the evidence of Dr James, even if he had raised a real*

possibility (which he did not) of search and restraint being a contributing cause of death. Her failure to call Dr James was therefore not unlawful.

44. In Lewis the Court of Appeal held that the coroner has a power but not a duty to leave to the jury in a Middleton inquest circumstances which were possible but not probable causes of death. Sedley LJ was 'unable to find a reason of principle for making it a duty'. Etherton LJ concluded that only matters which probably had a causal connection to death could form part of a verdict. There is therefore no requirement in a Middleton inquest to leave questions to a jury in respect of matters which possibly caused or contributed to the death.

And at paragraph 55:

"*55. The claimants' submission that all possible issues should be investigated relied upon the decision of the European Court of Human Rights in Mammadov v Azerbaijan Application No.4762/05, 17 March 2010. There the Court found the domestic investigation inadequate 'as it failed to seek answers to all the issues relevant for an assessment of the State agents' role' (at [123]). The key word there is 'relevant', meaning relevant to the central issues in the inquiry and not all possible issues and certainly not one (as here) which did not arise on the evidence.*"

R (Allen) v HM Coroner for Inner North London (2009) EWCA Civ 263

The deceased had been detained by an NHS trust as a mental patient. She was subsequently found by a nurse collapsed on a bathroom floor. A senior house officer was called and cardio-pulmonary resuscitation was administered. An ambulance then took S to a hospital where she was pronounced dead. A post-mortem report stated the cause of death was coronary artery disease leading to cardiac arrest.

The coroner confirmed that the disease that caused the death was coronary artery disease and concluded that the deceased died from natural causes.

The appellant was the husband of the deceased. He complained that the scope of the inquest was insufficient to satisfy the requirements of the European Convention on Human Rights 1950 art.2.

R applied for permission to judicially review the C's decisions at inquest. His application was refused on the basis that a broader inquest of the kind required by art.2 was not necessary as art.2 was not engaged and, even if art.2 was engaged, the inquiry was not deficient in any respects.

He then appealed that refusal.

In dismissing the appeal, the Court disagreed with the lower court that Article 2 was not engaged. However, in relation to the scope of the investigation undertaken by the coroner, it was not incumbent on him to investigate and state his conclusion in relation to every issue raised. The coroner was required to do no more than focus the investigation and the inquisition on the central issue or issues in the case.

It might have been preferable if C had investigated the oxygen cylinder issue since it had been raised in an internal inquiry report. However, it was clear that he would have concluded that it did not cause or contribute to S's death. S had died of coronary artery disease and nothing could have been done to save her.

<u>R (Parkinson) v Kent Senior Coroner (2018) EWHC 1501</u>

The claimant's mother had died, aged 91, in the Accident and Emergency department of a hospital run by the first interested party NHS trust. At the inquest, the coroner concluded that the cause of death was natural causes due to 'bronchopneumonia combined possibly with right lung pulmonary thrombi' and that no action reasonably taken by the hospital could have changed the outcome because she was in the advanced stages of dying when she arrived. He found no evidence of neglect in her treatment and he did not accept that the inquest should be an Article 2 inquest.

The claimant applied for a judicial review of the coroner's decision.

In refusing the application, the Court held at paragraphs 84 to 89:

> "*84. The primary substantive positive obligation [of A2] is to have in place a regulatory framework compelling hospitals, whether private or public, to adopt appropriate measures for the protection of patients' lives.*
>
> *85. The primary procedural obligation is to have a system of law in place, whether criminal or civil, by which individual failures can be the subject of an appropriate remedy. In the law of England and Wales that is achieved by having a criminal justice system, which can in principle hold to account a healthcare professional who causes a patient's death by gross negligence; and a civil justice system, which makes available a possible civil claim for negligence.*
>
> *86. The enhanced duty of investigation, which falls upon the state itself to initiate an effective and independent investigation, will only arise in medical cases in limited circumstances, where there is an arguable breach of the state's own substantive obligations under Article 2.*
>
> *87. Where the state has made adequate provision for securing high professional standards among health professionals and the protection of the lives of patients, matters such as an error of judgment on the part of a health professional or negligent coordination among health professionals in the treatment of a particular patient are not sufficient of themselves to call the state to account under Article 2*
>
> *88. However, there may be exceptional cases which go beyond mere error or medical negligence, in which medical staff, in breach of their professional obligations, fail to provide emergency medical treatment despite being fully aware that a person's life would be put at risk if that treatment is not given. In such a case the failure will result from a*

> *dysfunction in the hospital's services and this will be a structural issue linked to the deficiencies in the regulatory framework.*
>
> *89. At the risk of over-simplification, the crucial distinction is between a case where there is reason to believe that there may have been a breach which is a "systemic failure", in contrast to an "ordinary" case of medical negligence.*

And at paragraph 91:

> *91. Finally, we remind ourselves [in this context that Smith LJ said, at para. 71], that care should be taken to ensure that allegations of what are in truth allegations of "individual negligence" are not "dressed up as systemic failures"; and, at para. 72, that the person best placed to decide whether Article 2 is engaged is the coroner who conducts the inquest."*

<u>R (Morahan) v West London Assistnat Coroner (2021) EWHC 1603</u>

The deceased had a history of mental illness and had been an in-patient at a rehabilitation unit. She was initially detained under the Mental Health Act 1983 s.3, but subsequently was a voluntary in-patient. She had left the unit one day with her clinician's agreement but failed to return that evening as required. She was found dead six days later from a drugs overdose.

The coroner conducted pre-inquest reviews and held that there was no requirement for an Article 2 inquest.

The coroner found that there had been no state assumption of responsibility as the deceased was a voluntary patient and that there was no evidence of a real or immediate risk of which the Trust or the police should have been aware.

The claimant submitted that the circumstances of the deceased's death gave rise to an automatic duty to conduct such an inquest because there had been arguable breaches of a substantive operational duty owed by the

Trust to take steps to avert the real and immediate risk of her death by accidental drug overdose.

In refusing the application for judicial review, the Court held as follows.

The existence of the operational duty was not to be analysed solely by reference to the relationship between the state and the individual, but also, importantly, by reference to the type of harm of which the individual was foreseeably at real and immediate risk. There might be an operational duty to protect against some hazards but not others. Where vulnerable people were cared for by an institution which exercised control over them, whether an operational duty was owed to protect them from a foreseeable risk of a particular type of harm was informed by whether the nature of the control and harm were linked. For example, voluntary mental patients at risk of suicide had an impaired capacity to make a rational decision as to whether to take their own life, so their residence was not truly voluntary. There was, in such a case, a link between the nature of the control and the harm.

There was a duty on the state to investigate every death. In certain circumstances, there was also a distinct and additional enhanced duty of investigation. The duty was procedural and parasitic on a substantive duty. It arose whenever there was an arguable breach of the state's substantive art.2 duties and, in certain circumstances, automatically. In this case, the duty never arose automatically in the absence of an arguable breach of a substantive obligation.

(*Obiter*) Even if the above conclusion was wrong, there was in any event no automatic enhanced investigative duty in respect of an accidental death of a voluntary psychiatric patient.

R (Patton) v Assistant Coroner for Carmarthenshire & Pembrokeshire (2022) EWHC 1377 (Admin)

The Claimant applied to judicially review a coroner's decision not to make the inquest into the death of her daughter into an Article 2 inquest.

The claimant and her family, including daughter, had lived in Wales. In 2018 the claimant noticed that her daughter's behaviour had changed, particularly after she started using drugs. Accordingly, she was referred for specialist child adolescent mental health services.

In June 2019 the claimant's daughter moved in with a friend whose mother allowed her to use cannabis at their home. The claimant contacted the local authority and raised issues about her daughter being allowed to smoke cannabis where she was living, her mental health issues and the fact that she had taken an overdose in May 2018. She also sought assistance from the police.

On 23 October 2019, K was reported missing. Her body was found the following day. She had taken her own life.

Under the Social Services and Well-being (Wales) Act 2014 Pt 6 s.76(1)(c), the loc al authority had a duty to provide accommodation for any child within its area who appeared to it to require accommodation where the person who had been caring for the child had been prevented from providing the child with suitable accommodation or care. Under s.76(3) a local authority had to provide accommodation for any child within its area who had reached the age of 16 and whose well-being the local authority considered was likely to be seriously prejudiced if it did not provide the child with accommodation. A child who was provided with accommodation by the local authority in exercise of the s.76 duties was a "looked after child". The duties under s.76 were a restatement of those in the Children Act 1989 s.20.

An inquest was opened. The coroner held that there was no arguable case that the local authority had fallen short of its statutory responsibilities under s.76, and so Article 2 did not arise.

In granting the application for judicial review, the Court held as follows.

The coroner's reasons for ruling that the s.76(1)(c) duty did not apply were that (a) the deceased actually had accommodation at her friend's home; and (b) the local authority did not consider her to be homeless or requiring accommodation. As to (a), there were good arguments to the effect that the fact that the deceased actually had accommodation did not negate the potential s.76(1)(c) duty if the accommodation was unsuitable. The coroner erred by not engaging with that issue. As to (b) the views of one of the parties as to whether a child was in fact looked after were not determinative, and the court had to conduct its own assessment of whether a child should have been considered as such. The brevity of the coroner's reasons made it hard to discern that he had undertaken that exercise.

The coroner had not given adequate reasons for his finding in respect of s.76(3)(c); he simply re-stated the statutory test in s.76(3)(c). He gave no reasons for his decision that no obligation arose. The main point advanced by the claimant was that the accommodation where K was permitted to smoke cannabis, despite her mental health issues, would seriously prejudice her well-being. Accordingly, that was the principal important controversial issue and it was therefore, incumbent on the coroner to explain, even in brief terms, how he had resolved it.

<u>R (Gorani) v Assistant Coroner for West London (2022) EWHC 1593</u>

The deceased had jumped to his death from the balcony of his family home in December 2018. Prior to his death he had been diagnosed by his GP as suffering from depression and was prescribed with anti-depressants and had attempted suicide once before.

During the inquest the coroner rejected the applicant's submission that she should recuse herself on grounds of bias.

The applicant submitted that (1) the inquest had been procedurally/substantively unfair as the coroner had substituted her own evidence for those of the witnesses, that her questioning and general demeanour had given the appearance of bias and that she had erred by not recusing herself from the proceedings; (2) the coroner had failed to discharge the investigative obligation in ECHR art.2; (3) the coroner had made material errors of fact or failed to take material evidence into account; (4) the coroner had erred in law by deciding that a Regulation 28 (Preventing Future Deaths) report (see chapter 14 for discussion about these types of reports) was not required, without first hearing submissions from the interested parties.

The application was refused. In relation to bias, the Court held that the test of bias was whether a fair-minded observer, having considered the facts would conclude that there was a real possibility of bias. There was absolutely nothing in the transcript to support such a conclusion.

At paragraph 29:

> *"29. On the face of it, there was a perfectly adequate system in place here, as the Coroner had concluded on 25 June 2020; the problem was with the operation of the system on this particular occasion, a circumstance that will generally not engage Article 2."*

And at paragraphs 66 to 72:

> *"66. … I deal first with [counsel for the Claimant's] approach to Article 2 generally. Inherent in his submissions is the argument that once the coroner had declared that the inquest was to be " an Article 2 inquest ", all aspects of the Article 2 jurisdiction were in play. I would reject that suggestion, and would make the following five points.*
>
> *67. First, the fact that a coroner declares that an inquest will serve to meet the state's obligation to investigate the death, and that s5(2) of the 2009 Act applies, does not trigger an obligation on the coroner to investigate every aspect of the case to the standards of Article 2. The obligation imposed by s5(2) requires an investigation " where necessary " to ensure compliance with the Convention. A coroner's ruling as to the particular issues in respect of which Article 2 requires investigation delimits the scope of the Article 2 inquiry. Here, the scope of the*

investigation necessary to discharge the Article 2 obligation – namely to determine whether there was a breach of the system duty on 12 December – was never amended or challenged. And it was on that issue that the coroner properly focused her conclusions.

68. Second, the scope of the inquest is, and remains throughout, a matter for the coroner ...

70. Third, the significance of the ruling that Article 2 applies lies in the conclusion that will be reached at the end of the inquest. The " scope of the investigation and thus evidence called at the inquest is unlikely to be affected by the question whether the article 2 procedural obligation applies ", (Maguire v HM Senior Coroner for Blackpool & Fylde [2020] EWCA Civ 738). The Coroner here determined that Article 2 required an investigation into the alleged breach of the systems duty on 12 December 2018.

71. Fourth, the Coroner is not obliged to investigate every issue raised by an interested party...

72. Fifth, [counsel for the Claimant's] skeleton argument made frequent reference to caselaw relating to the operational duty owed to prisoners and those held in psychiatric hospitals; (R (Takoushis) v Inner North London Coroner [2005] EWCA Civ 1440, Mitchell v Glasgow CC [2009] 1 AC 874, Sacker v Coroner [2004] 1 WLR 796 and others.) But these have little or no relevance to cases such as the present, where what is in issue is the systems duty in respect of healthcare in the community."

<u>R (Maguire) v HM Senior Coroner for Blackpool and Fylde (2023) UKSC 20</u>

The appellants daughter had died in hospital as a result of a perforated gastric ulcer, peritonitis and pneumonia. She had Down's syndrome, learning disabilities and behavioural difficulties. She lacked capacity to make decisions about her living arrangements, healthcare and welfare and lived in a residential care home. Her placement was supervised and funded by the local authority.

The deceased fell ill at the home and an ambulance was called. Although the paramedics wanted to take her to hospital, she refused to go. On the advice of a GP, therefore, she was permitted to remain in the home overnight. By the next day her condition had worsened and she was taken to hospital, where she died.

The coroner refused to make the inquest an Article 2 inquest. He considered that there had been no failure by the care home or the ambulance service to have appropriate systems in place. Therefore the enhanced procedural obligation was not engaged as what was being alleged amounted to no more than medical negligence by healthcare staff.

The jury concluded that J died of natural causes. The appellant unsuccessfully applied for judicial review of the coroner's decision in relation to scope.

The case ultimately made its way to the Supreme Court.

In dismissing the appeal, the Court held that there had been no arguable breach of the systems duty by the care home such as to trigger the enhanced procedural obligation. At paragraph 146:

> "*146. It is clear that the systems in place at the care home were capable of being operated in a way which would ensure that a proper standard of care was provided to residents at the home, even though there may have been individual lapses in putting them into effect. As explained in Humberstone, para 71, and Parkinson , para 91, individual lapses in putting a proper system into effect are not to be confused with a deficiency in the system itself.*"

At paragraph 190:

> "*190. When an individual is placed in a care home, a nursing home or a hospital, the state's operational duty [in the targeted sense derived*

from Osman , para 116,] does not involve an assumption of responsibility extending to taking responsibility for all aspects of their physical health, with the consequence that if he or she dies from some medical condition which was not diagnosed and treated in time the state's duty is engaged and the enhanced procedural obligation in terms of accountability is triggered. Even though the individual may not be at liberty, the state is not for that reason made the guarantor of the adequacy of healthcare provided to them in all respects, with an enhanced obligation to account if things go wrong. That would not be consistent with the established approach in relation to cases of alleged medical negligence and the approach adopted in the suicide risk cases discussed above."

And at paragraphs 207 to 208:

"207. Also, as a general matter, healthcare professionals should seek to respect the autonomy of those in their care where possible and should at all times aim to act in their best interests, avoiding harm to them. Where an ambulance crew encounter a patient who is resistant to going to hospital, it is not a simple matter to say they must be forced to go either by means of physical restraint or by chemical restraint through the administration of sedatives. Both may have negative effects which harm the patient. An assessment is called for, to ensure that if such means are to be used, that is only where this is proportionate to the risk faced by the patient.

208. None of the healthcare professionals involved was on notice that Jackie's life was in danger, so as to engage the Osman operational duty. Furthermore, the paramedics, who had the ultimate decision about taking Jackie to hospital (albeit with the benefit of medical advice given by Dr Fairhead) gave proper consideration to the question whether she ought to be removed there and made an assessment which was reasonable in the circumstances, that the risk to her was not so great as to make that appropriate. At the inquest, the relevant expert witness (Dr Goode) did not criticise them for making this decision".

CHAPTER SEVEN

SHOULD THERE BE A JURY?

The vast majority of inquests do not have a jury; indeed, the government statistics for 2022 indicate that only 1% of inquests that year were held with a jury[6]. However, considering that virtually all inquests with a jury will tend to include advocates, the average inquest practitioner may well act in at least one inquest with a jury during their career.

There are two situations in the law which allow for an inquest to be held with a jury:

(i) Where the coroner has a duty to hold the inquest with a jury under section 7(2) of the 2009 Act;

(ii) Where the coroner has a discretion to hold the inquest with a jury under section 7(3) of the 2009 Act.

The question as to whether there should be a jury in a given inquest is usually determined at a pre-inquest stage, but can be decided at any stage during the course of the inquest.

DUTY TO HOLD AN INQUEST WITH A JURY

Section 7(2) of the 2009 Act sets out the circumstances in which an inquest **must** be held with a jury.

---

[6] Available at https://www.gov.uk/government/statistics/coroners-statistics-2022/coroners-statistics-2022-england-and-wales#:~:text=Coroners%20can%20exercise%20discretionary%20powers,%2Dyear%20pre%2Dpandemic%20average, last accessed on 5 October 2023

2) An inquest into a death must be held with a jury if the senior coroner has reason to suspect—

(a) that the deceased died while in custody or otherwise in state detention, and that either—

(i) the death was a violent or unnatural one, or

(ii) the cause of death is unknown,

(b) that the death resulted from an act or omission of—

(i) a police officer, or

(ii) a member of a service police force,

in the purported execution of the officer's or member's duty as such, or

(c) that the death was caused by a notifiable accident, poisoning or disease."

REASON TO SUSPECT

The phrase 'the coroner has reason to suspect' is similar to the test under section 8 of the previous Act (the Coroners Act 1988) 'if it appears to the coroner'.

The threshold is a low one and does not require proof positive or even formulated evidence (*R v Inner London Coroner ex parte Linnane* (1989) 1 WLR 395 at 398). However, the coroner must properly apply his or her mind to the question or risk their decision being overturned on judicial review. In *R (Aineto) v HM Coroner for Brighton and Hove* (2003) EWHC 1896 (Admin) at paragraphs 11 to 12:

"*11. I would therefore hold that in this case the defendant had reason to suspect that the conditions of section 8(3)(c)* [of the 1988 Act] *were satisfied and that she erred in failing to summon a jury. I should add that there is no evidence that she in fact applied her mind to this question. Miss Hewitt submits that we should infer that she must have done so. In her second witness statement the defendant says:*

> *"As I stated in paragraph 3 of my first statement, when I was first informed of Mr Aineto's death, on the 31st July 2001, I was also made aware that he had apparently been killed when in contact with a rubbish collection dustcart. In view of the involvement of the dustcart I did consider that this was a case which the Health and Safety Executive ("HSE") may wish to investigate itself. Within two or three days I therefore asked my officer, Theresa Bromage, to inform the HSE of the death. I do not hesitate to involve the HSE in appropriate cases, and I find their investigations and attendance at inquests are of great assistance.*
>
> *Mrs Bromage reported to me that she had contacted the HSE by telephone and had informed them of Mr Aineto's death and its circumstances. They indicated to her, during the conversation that they did not need to become involved in the investigation. I knew the events surrounding the death would be thoroughly investigated by the Police Crash Investigation Unit, and that I would be able to hear evidence of that investigation at the inquest. However, had that police investigation or any other evidence which subsequently came to my attention made me think that the HSE ought to be contacted again, then I would not have hesitated to have done this, as I have in the past."*

12. There is an issue as to whether the HSE were in fact so notified. It seems clear that there was no formal notification. However that may be, it seems that even on her own evidence the defendant considered notifying the HSE only in order to see whether they should be involved in the investigation. In this respect, no doubt, she had Rule 23 in mind. But it does not follow from this that she considered the section 8(3)(c) question. If she had done so, I would have expected her to say so in terms and explain why she considered at the time that there was no reason to suspect that the death was caused by a reportable accident."

This case also made clear that where the High Court finds that a coroner has wrongly decided not to call a jury, then a fresh inquest must be ordered unless there are "*cogent reasons to deny a fresh inquest*" (paragraph 12 of *Aineto*).

DEFINITION OF 'STATE DETENTION'

Section 48(2) and (2A) of the 2009 Act assists us with understanding the definition of 'state detention':

> "*(2) Subject to subsection (2A), a person is in state detention if he or she is compulsorily detained by a public authority within the meaning of section 6 of the Human Rights Act 1998 (c. 42).*
>
> *(2A) But a person is not in state detention at any time when he or she is deprived of liberty under section 4A(3) or (5) or 4B of the Mental Capacity Act 2005.*"

This makes it clear that a person is not considered to be in 'state detention' when they are in custody of the State but are not compulsorily detained. For example, a person who is a voluntary patient in a hospital will not be considered to have been in 'state detention' for the purposes of the 2009 Act. This ties in with the decision of the Court of Appeal in *Rabbone v Pennine Care NHS Foundation Trust* (2010) EWCA Civ 698 that Article 2 was not engaged in the case of a voluntary hospital patient.

Interestingly, though, section (2A) (which was only added to the 2009 Act in 2017 by virtue of the Policing and Crime Act of that year) makes clear that 'state detention' does not include compulsory detention for medical purposes under the Mental Capacity Act 2005.

DEFINITION OF NOTIFIABLE ACCIDENT, POISONING OR DISEASE

Section 7(4) and (5) of the 2009 Act define what is considered a 'notifiable accident, poisoning or disease' for the purposes of inquests.

> "*(4) For the purposes of subsection (2)(c) an accident, poisoning or disease is "notifiable" if notice of it is required under any Act to be given—*
>
> > *(a) to a government department,*
> >
> > *(b) to an inspector or other officer of a government department, or*
> >
> > *(c) to an inspector appointed under section 19 of the Health and Safety at Work etc. Act 1974 (c. 37).*
>
> *(5) But COVID-19 is not a notifiable disease for the purposes of subsection (2)(c).*"

Covid-19 is specifically not a notifiable disease for the purposes of the 2009 Act. The Coronavirus Act 2020 makes clear that this decision is for policy reasons, to avoid inquests becoming overwhelmed in the aftermath of the 2020 pandemic:

> "*66. Under existing legislation, the status of COVID-19 as a notifiable disease in England meant that any inquest into a death where the coroner has reason to suspect that the death was caused by COVID-19 must take place with a jury.*
>
> *67. This could have very significant resource implications for coroner workload and Local Authority coroner services, resulting in a possible 25,000 additional jury inquests even at the lower end of COVID-19 mortality modelling in England and Wales.*

68. Although the inquests could be adjourned until the pandemic has passed, this would deprive bereaved families of swift closure and would, in any event, simply delay resource pressure for the future.

69. The Act modifies the existing legislation to disapply the requirement that coroners must conduct any inquest with a jury where they have reason to suspect the death was caused by COVID-19. For Northern Ireland, the Act makes corresponding provision, including in relation to inquests into a death in prison from natural illness."

From 28 June 2024, the 2009 Act will be amended again to remove reference to Covid-19 in this section of the Act.

DISCRETION TO CALL A JURY

Section 7(3) of the 2009 Act provides the coroner with a statutory discretion to hold an inquest with a jury:

"*(3) An inquest into a death may be held with a jury if the senior coroner thinks that there is sufficient reason for doing so.*"

This is a broad discretion. Of course, the coroner's decision should still be reasonable and take into account relevant factors without paying regard to irrelevant factors (see Chapter 15 for more detail about the grounds for judicial review).

RELEVANT CASES

R v Inner North London Coroner ex p Linnane (1989) 1 WLR 395

Mr Linnane had been sentenced to a term of imprisonment, but because of overcrowding he was in fact being held in a police station. He suffered from both epilepsy and alcoholism, which even to non-medics might strike you as a dangerous combination. During the evening of 8 October 1988, his son visited him and found him naked except for a paper towel around his waist. He was shaking and his lips were blue. His son said to the police officers that his father needed hospital attention. He evidently wasn't listened to at that stage because later on, Mr Linnane was still in his cell when he was found unconscious.

Mr Linnane was transported to hospital by police officers after an ambulance was called but failed to arrive. The cause of death was acute myocarditis

An inquest was held, but the coroner declined to hold the inquest with a jury. The decision of the coroner was judicially reviewed

The Divisional Court granted an order of mandamus – a mandatory order – to compel the coroner to empanel a jury. This is a pre 2009 Act case, so was based on some now defunct law in the 1988 statute. Essentially in that old statute the coroner was mandated to empanel a jury where a person was in police custody and there was the continuance or possible recurrence of the circumstances which were prejudicial to the health and safety of the public

But this is an interesting and useful case because of its discussion about what is meant in the legislation by 'the coroner has reason to suspect'.

At 398D:

> *"…the phrase which is the preamble to the specific provisions … 'there is reason to suspect', does not require positive proof or even formulated evidence. The question is usually to be decided at a preliminary stage although, as indicated in the subsection, it may arise for decision during the inquest. Therefore, any information giving 'reason to suspect' will suffice."*

<u>R (Ferreira) v HM Senior Coroner for South London (2017) EWCA Civ 31</u>

The deceased had Down's syndrome and learning difficulties. She had been admitted to intensive care with pneumonia and heart problems. She was intubated and sedated but died following a cardiac arrest. The hospital had not sought any authorisation for depriving M of her liberty under the Mental Capacity Act 2005 and had not admitted her under the Mental Health Act 1983. The coroner considered that it was necessary to hold an inquest into M's death, but decided to do so without a jury, finding that the deceased had not been in "state detention" under the Coroners and Justice Act 2009 s.7.

The appellant submitted that the coroner was obliged to hold an inquest with a jury under s.7 because the deceased's hospital treatment meant that she had been deprived of her liberty and had therefore been in "state detention". She argued that the deceased had been under the continuous control and supervision of the hospital.

The appeal was dismissed; the Court of Appeal finding that a hospital stay did not constitute 'state detention' for the purposes of section 2)(a) of the 2009 Act. A death in intensive care was not, in the absence of special circumstances, a death in "state detention" for the purposes of the 2009 Act. Treatment in an intensive care unit was not, in general, appropriately treated as a deprivation of liberty. To require authorisation of the deprivation of liberty in a normal intensive care case would involve a significant dilution of clinical resources, time and attention, which would risk jeopardising the outcome for all intensive care patients. The coroner's decision had been correct in law.

The Court noted that if a patient in an intensive care unit tried to leave, it was likely that the clinicians would try to persuade them not to but there was no evidence that they would go so far as to prevent them. In other words, there was continuous supervision and control, but there was not lack of freedom to leave.

CHAPTER EIGHT

EVIDENCE

The coroner has ultimate responsibility for marshalling and disclosing the evidence. The coroner will consider evidence provided to him or her (which can be from interested persons, witnesses or other sources) and then determine what is relevant to the inquest and should be disclosed to interested persons. The coroner will also make decisions as to disclosure of the evidence to the public.

The law in relation to disclosure is set out within the statute, with additional guidance to be found in the Chief Coroner's Guidance Notes and Law Sheets. In addition, the leading case on disclosure is *Worcestershire County Council & Anor v HM Coroner for the County of Worcestershire* (2013) EWHC 1711 (QB), a comprehensive analysis of which is in the 'Cases' section below.

DISCLOSURE OF EVIDENCE TO INTERESTED PERSONS

Rule 13 of the 2013 Inquests Rules provides:

> "***13.— Disclosure of documents at the request of an interested person***
>
> *(1) Subject to rule 15, where an interested person asks for disclosure of a document held by the coroner, the coroner must provide that document or a copy of that document, or make the document available for inspection by that person as soon as is reasonably practicable.*
>
> *(2) Documents to which this rule applies include—*
>
> *(a) any post-mortem examination report;*

> *(b) any other report that has been provided to the coroner during the course of the investigation;*
>
> *(c) where available, the recording of any inquest hearing held in public, but not in relation to any part of the hearing from which the public was excluded under rule 11(4) or (5);*
>
> *(d) any other document which the coroner considers relevant to the inquest.*"

The caveat in Rule 15 is as follows:

> "***15. Restrictions on disclosure***
>
> *A coroner may refuse to provide a document or a copy of a document requested under rule 13 where—*
>
> > *(a) there is a statutory or legal prohibition on disclosure;*
> >
> > *(b) the consent of any author or copyright owner cannot reasonably be obtained;*
> >
> > *(c) the request is unreasonable;*
> >
> > *(d) the document relates to contemplated or commenced criminal proceedings; or*
> >
> > *(e) the coroner considers the document irrelevant to the investigation.*"

Guidance No.44 *Disclosure* sets out key principles in relation to the way that the coroner gathers and discloses evidence.

Paragraph 3 sets out the following key points:

- Marshalling evidence is a judicial function;

- Evidence needs to be relevant, reasonable, sufficient and proportionate to the scope of the inquest;

- The coroner should set clear dates for disclosure of material, and should monitor and act upon any non-compliance;

- Paragraph 1 of Schedule 5 to the Coroners and Justice Act 2009 gives a coroner the power, by way of a written notice, to compel the production of evidence for the purposes of an investigation;

- Coroners should only use Schedule 5 notices to compel disclosure where the disclosure is necessary and, unless there are exceptional circumstances, should attempt to obtain the disclosure by agreement before issuing a notice;

- The General Medical Council has issued guidance on confidentiality which confirms that doctors should disclose information to help a coroner with an inquest.

Deciding what to disclose is a judicial decision (paragraph 5 of Guidance No.44). Guidance No.44 confirms at paragraph 11 that whilst information needs to be disclosed as soon as reasonably practicable by virtue of the 2013 Inquests Rules, it may be reasonable to provide disclosure "*as a bundle rather than piecemeal, depending on the circumstances of the case*".

Where there are pre-inquest review hearings the interested persons should be given sufficient disclosure of relevant statements and documents before the hearing so that they can address the agenda on an informed basis (paragraph 12 of Guidance No.44).

DISCLOSURE OF EVIDENCE TO THE PUBLIC

Regulation 27(2) of the Investigation Regulations 2013 provides:

> "*(2) The coroner may provide any document or copy of any document to any person who in the opinion of the coroner is a proper person to have possession of it.*"

Chief Coroner's Guidance No.25 *Coroners and the Media* indicates the following factors that the coroner should take into account in relation to such a request (paragraph 28):

- The person requesting the document;
- The reason for the request;
- The public interest;
- The sensitivities of particular passages of evidence;
- The need for editing or redaction (if any); and
- Other relevant factors.

Guidance No.25 does make clear, at paragraph 29, that "*although coroners have a discretion on this point, members of the media (who can show identification where necessary) should normally be expected to be considered proper persons for these purposes*".

POWER OF THE CORONER TO COMPEL DISCLOSURE OF EVIDENCE AND ATTENDANCE OF WITNESSES

POWER OF COMPULSION

The Coroner does have powers to compel the disclosure of evidence and the attendance of witnesses under Schedule 5 of the 2009 Act.

Paragraphs 1 and 2 of Schedule 5 to the 2009 Act state as follows:

Paragraph 1

"*1*

(1) A senior coroner may by notice require a person to attend at a time and place stated in the notice and—

(a) to give evidence at an inquest,

(b) to produce any documents in the custody or under the control of the person which relate to a matter that is relevant to an inquest, or

(c) to produce for inspection, examination or testing any other thing in the custody or under the control of the person which relates to a matter that is relevant to an inquest.

(2) A senior coroner who is conducting an investigation under this Part may by notice require a person, within such period as the senior coroner thinks reasonable—

(a) to provide evidence to the senior coroner, about any matters specified in the notice, in the form of a written statement,

(b) to produce any documents in the custody or under the control of the person which relate to a matter that is relevant to the investigation, or

(c) to produce for inspection, examination or testing any other thing in the custody or under the control of the person which relates to a matter that is relevant to the investigation.

(3) A notice under sub-paragraph (1) or (2) must—

(a) explain the possible consequences, under paragraphs 6 and 7 of Schedule 6, of not complying with the notice;

(b) indicate what the recipient of the notice should do if he or she wishes to make a claim under sub-paragraph (4).

(4) A claim by a person that—

(a) he or she is unable to comply with a notice under this paragraph, or

(b) it is not reasonable in all the circumstances to require him or her to comply with such a notice,

is to be determined by the senior coroner, who may revoke or vary the notice on that ground.

(5) In deciding whether to revoke or vary a notice on the ground mentioned in sub-paragraph (4)(b), the senior coroner must consider the public interest in the information in question being obtained for the purposes of the inquest or investigation, having regard to the likely importance of the information.

(6) For the purposes of this paragraph a document or thing is under a person's control if it is in the person's possession or if he or she has a right to possession of it.

(7) The validity of a notice under sub-paragraph (1) or (2) is not limited to the coroner area for which the senior coroner issuing the notice is appointed.

(8) A reference in this paragraph to a senior coroner is to be read as including the Coroner for Treasure. As it applies in relation to the Coroner for Treasure, this paragraph has effect with the omission of sub-paragraph (7)."

Paragraph 2

"*2*

(1) A person may not be required to give, produce or provide any evidence or document under paragraph 1 if—

(a) he or she could not be required to do so in civil proceedings in a court in England and Wales, or

(b) the requirement would be incompatible with [a retained EU obligation]1.

(2) The rules of law under which evidence or documents are permitted or required to be withheld on grounds of public interest immunity apply in relation to an investigation or inquest under this Part as they apply in relation to civil proceedings in a court in England and Wales."

Remember, though, that paragraph 3 of Guidance No.44 makes clear that this is a power to be used where the disclosure is necessary and the Coroner has attempted to obtain disclosure by agreement first.

This is spelled out in more detail in the Chief Coroner's Guide to the 2009 Act at paragraph 133:

"*Coroners should not be too hasty to exercise these powers. They should only be used where necessary and where other methods have failed. Much can be achieved by agreement with, for example, local hospitals, on regular procedures for the production of witness statements, medical notes and reports.*"

And in Guidance No.9 (relating to Openings), the Chief Coroner states at paragraph 37:

> *"In this context, at openings, coroners should not normally use the power to require evidence to be produced under Schedule 5 of the 2009 Act. Schedule 5 should not in any event be used too freely. It is something to be used when other methods of request have failed, bearing in mind that the notice to produce under Schedule 5 must include the possible penal consequences for non-compliance (see Schedule 6). Summonses, the equivalent in civil and criminal courts, are not used routinely."*

SANCTIONS FOR NON-COMPLIANCE WITH SCHEDULE 5

Schedule 6 sets out the various offences which can be committed in the inquest context. The majority relate to jurors, but paragraphs 6 to 8 inclusive relate to non-compliance with a direction of the coroner under Schedule 5.

Paragraph 6 provides the coroner with the power to impose a fine on a person who fails without reasonable excuse to comply with a direction under paragraph 1 of Schedule 5. Paragraph 7 creates offences for intentionally destroying or concealing evidence. Paragraph 8 creates offences in relation to providing false evidence.

<u>Paragraph 6</u>

> "*6*
>
> *A senior coroner, or (as the case may be) the Coroner for Treasure, may impose a fine not exceeding £1000 on a person who fails without reasonable excuse to do anything required by a notice under paragraph 1 of Schedule 5.*"

Paragraph 7

"7

(1) It is an offence for a person to do anything that is intended to have the effect of—

(a) distorting or otherwise altering any evidence, document or other thing that is given, produced or provided for the purposes of an investigation under this Part of this Act, or

(b) preventing any evidence, document or other thing from being given, produced or provided for the purposes of such an investigation,

or to do anything that the person knows or believes is likely to have that effect.

(2) It is an offence for a person—

(a) intentionally to suppress or conceal a document that is, and that the person knows or believes to be, a relevant document, or

(b) intentionally to alter or destroy such a document.

(3) For the purposes of sub-paragraph (2) a document is a "relevant document" if it is likely that a person conducting an investigation under this Part of this Act would (if aware of its existence) wish to be provided with it.

(4) A person does not commit an offence under sub-paragraph (1) or (2) by doing anything that is authorised or required—

(a) by a senior coroner or the Coroner for Treasure, or

(b) by virtue of paragraph 2 of Schedule 5 or any privilege that applies.

(5) Proceedings for an offence under sub-paragraph (1) or (2) may be instituted only by or with the consent of the Director of Public Prosecutions.

(6) A person guilty of an offence under sub-paragraph (1) or (2) is liable on summary conviction to a fine not exceeding level 3 on the standard scale, or to imprisonment for a term not exceeding 51 weeks, or to both."

Para 8

"*8*

(1) It is an offence for a person, in giving unsworn evidence at an inquest by virtue of section 45(2)(a), to give false evidence in such circumstances that, had the evidence been given on oath, he or she would have been guilty of perjury.

(2) A person guilty of an offence under this paragraph is liable on summary conviction to a fine not exceeding £1000, or to imprisonment for a term not exceeding 51 weeks, or to both.

(3) In relation to a person under the age of 14, sub-paragraph (2) has effect as if for the words following "summary conviction" there were substituted "to a fine not exceeding £250".

(4) For the purposes of sub-paragraph (3), a person's age is to be taken to be that which it appears to the court to be after considering any available evidence."

RELEVANT CASES

Worcestershire County Council & Anor v HM Coroner for the County of Worcestershire (2013) EWHC 1711 (QB)

This is a key case in the context of disclosure.

The coroner had adjourned an inquest into the death of a 16-year-old child in foster care who had been found hanged. The second claimant board undertook a Serious Case Review (SCR) and obtained a number of Individual Management Reviews (IMRs) and Information Reports (IRs) from the various agencies contributing to D's care. It produced a draft SCR overview report pending the outcome of the inquest. The coroner requested a copy of the draft report, which the board provided, and copies of the IMRs and IRs, which the board declined to provide. The coroner obtained witness summonses requiring the provision of the documents under CPR r.34.3(2)(c) and r.34.4(1). The claimants sought to set aside the orders on the basis that the documents were protected by public interest immunity (PII) and/or their disclosure was unnecessary.

In refusing the application, the Court held that it was necessary to balance the perceived public benefit afforded by withholding the documents against the public benefit of disclosure. At paragraph 92 the Court listed a number of factors likely to subsist in such cases:

> "*92. In doing so, it is necessary to bear in mind a number of factors which are likely to subsist in such cases:*
>
> *i) HM Coroner has an equally crucial role in investigating suspicious deaths within his area, including the death of a "looked after" child who has died a "violent or unnatural death."*
>
> *ii) Subject to the supervisory jurisdiction of this court, the scope of an inquest is essentially a matter for the coroner, (Regina v HM Coroner for North Humberside and Scunthorpe ex-parte Jamieson , supra). Indeed in cases involving the death of a "looked after" child, and where an Article 2 type of inquiry is required, it may be that the State's*

procedural investigative obligations would not be satisfied by the SCR process, and would require that inquiry to be carried out in the context of a Middleton type inquest. (Plymouth City Council v Her Majesty's Coroner for the County of Devon (Plymouth and South West District) and the Secretary of State for Education and Skills, supra). Even where such an inquest is not required, the coroner's Rule 43 powers may require a fuller investigation into the circumstances in which the death occurred. Moreover, a Jamieson type inquest may require the investigation of systematic failures (The Queen (on the application of Butler) v HM Coroner for the Black Country District, supra).

iii) Reflecting the pre-eminent role of HM Coroner in deciding the scope of an inquest, this court will only interfere with such a decision in exceptional circumstances, (Regina v Inner West London Coroner ex-parte Dallaglio & Another , supra).

iv) The role of HM Coroner is not an adversarial one, but an investigative one, such that questions of relevance and necessity are unlikely to be as decisive as they would be in the context of civil litigation, (Inner West London Assistant Deputy Coroner v Channel Four Television Corporation, supra).

v) Where in the context of a claim of public interest immunity a balance has to be struck between competing public interests, it may be that because of the nature of his inquiry the balance ought normally to be in favour of disclosure to HM Coroner, (Re A subpoena (Adoption Commissioner for Local Administration, supra).

vi) What is sought is not disclosure of the IMRs and IRs to the public in general or indeed anyone else, save and except HM Coroner. Thus the argument in favour of non-disclosure arising out of the need to encourage openness within the IMRs and IRs is likely to be significantly diluted, (McCaughey (Judicial Review Application), supra). This being in contradistinction to the situation which may arise with the question of disclosure to members of the public (ICO Decision Notice

Plymouth City Council Reference FS50084360 and ICO Decision Notice London Borough of Haringey Reference FS50234513).

vii) The question of any further disclosure is a matter for HM Coroner, having taken into account any further arguments in favour of non-disclosure and subject to the supervisory jurisdiction of this court; thus maintaining sufficient safeguards to those properly seeking non-disclosure of these documents (Inner West London Assistant Deputy Coroner v Channel Four Television Corporation, supra)."

R (Ahmed) v South and East Cumbria Coroner (2009) EWHC 1653 Admin)

The claimant parents sought permission to apply for judicial review of the defendant coroner's decision not to disclose material prior to an inquest into the death of their 17-year-old daughter.

The deceased had disappeared from home and her body was later found in undergrowth. An inquest was opened following an inconclusive police investigation. A number of suspects had been interviewed, including the claimants and other family members. The claimants requested disclosure of all material prior to the inquest. The coroner replied that he would consider more specific requests, which were not forthcoming.

The application for judicial review was refused. The Court held that there was no hard-and-fast obligation on a coroner to disclose any witness statements or material; it was a matter of discretion. A more liberal approach had developed towards disclosure in inquest cases and it was often advisable that there should be disclosure of material central to the inquest. It would have been preferable, regardless of the lack of specificity of the requests, had the coroner chosen to disclose some of the key material, for example the statements of those witnesses he intended to call. However, the coroner's decision could not be characterised as unreasonable, given the ongoing investigation and the opportunity provided to the claimants to request specific disclosure.

The Court added that even if the discretion had not been properly exercised, a fresh inquest would not have been ordered: the claimants had been unable to show that there would have been any material difference to the outcome of the inquest if disclosure had been made.

Mack v HM Coroner for Birmingham (2011) EWCA Civ 712

The appellant appealed against the High Court's refusal of her application to quash the inquest into the death of her husband.

The deceased had gone into hospital to have a hip replacement. It was successful and he was discharged. A day later he began vomiting. He tested positive for the clostridium difficile infection. He later deteriorated and was taken into intensive care. He was dehydrated and had acute renal failure but responded to treatment. After nine days on the ward, M suffered a cardiac arrest and died. He was 77.

Before the inquest M's family gave the coroner an extensive list of witnesses whom they wanted called, and urged him to summon a jury pursuant to the Coroners Act 1988 s.8(3)(d) in light of their belief that problems with M's treatment amounted to systemic failures. The coroner declined to summon a jury, and did not call all the witnesses on the list. Notably, he only called one doctor, and nobody personally involved in the deceased's case in the last nine days of his life gave evidence.

In allowing the appeal, the Court held:

(1) This was not a case of one individual failing; there was a whole series of failings. The natural person to be asked to try and help explain them would have been somebody with some knowledge and responsibility for that ward. It was not that every case of a hospital death would require the evidence of a doctor from each ward where the patient might have been. Yet in the instant case, the medical witness could not answer questions relating to the practice on the ward in general. The coroner had given no rational explanation for saying that it was not appropriate to call

other witnesses to give evidence, given the variety and troubling nature of the many shortcomings.

At paragraphs 8 to 9:

> "*8. … The point was validly made that the coroner could not reasonably be expected to call every witness who might be able to give relevant evidence; that would have taken many medical witnesses away from their responsibilities for the treatment of patients. In any event, the matter is governed by law. Section 11 of the Coroners Act 1988 provides certain material:*
>
> > *"The Coroner shall, at the first sitting of the inquest, examine on oath touching the death all persons who tender their evidence respecting the facts and all persons having knowledge of the facts whom he thinks it expedient to examine."*
>
> *9. There is clear authority and it is not in dispute that this gives to the coroner a wide discretion – or perhaps more appropriately a wide area of judgment — whom it is expedient to call. The court will only intervene if satisfied that the decision made was one which was not properly open to him on Wednesbury principles.*"

(2) The remaining question of whether a jury should be summoned for the fresh inquest was for the coroner to decide in light of submissions made to him and with the knowledge of what changes had been made at the hospital since M died.

PART THREE

THE INQUEST HEARING

CHAPTER NINE

EVIDENCE IN WRITING AND INQUESTS ENTIRELY IN WRITING

POWER TO ADMIT ANY EVIDENCE IN WRITING

Rule 23 of the Coroners (Inquest) Rules 2013 allows for the coroner to admit any evidence in writing:

> "*23.— Written evidence*
>
> *(1) Written evidence as to who the deceased was and how, when and where the deceased came by his or her death is not admissible unless the coroner is satisfied that—*
>
> > *(a) it is not possible for the maker of the written evidence to give evidence at the inquest hearing at all, or within a reasonable time;*
> >
> > *(b) there is a good and sufficient reason why the maker of the written evidence should not attend the inquest hearing;*
> >
> > *(c) there is a good and sufficient reason to believe that the maker of the written evidence will not attend the inquest hearing; or*
> >
> > *(d) the written evidence (including evidence in admission form) is unlikely to be disputed.*
>
> *(2) Before admitting such written evidence the coroner must announce at the inquest hearing—*
>
> > *(a) what the nature of the written evidence to be admitted is;*

(b) the full name of the maker of the written evidence to be admitted in evidence;

(c) that any interested person may object to the admission of any such written evidence; and

(d) that any interested person is entitled to see a copy of any written evidence if he or she so wishes.

(3) A coroner must admit as evidence at an inquest hearing any document made by a deceased person if the coroner is of the opinion that the contents of the document are relevant to the purposes of the inquest.

(4) A coroner may direct that all or parts only of any written evidence submitted under this rule may be read aloud at the inquest hearing."

On 28 June 2022, Section 9C of the 2009 Act came into effect, allowing entire inquests to be held in written form.

Section 9C states:

"***9C Inquests without jury to be conducted at hearing or in writing***

(1) Where an inquest into a death is to be held without a jury, the inquest is to be held—

(a) at a hearing, or

(b) if the senior coroner decides that a hearing is unnecessary, in writing.

(2) The senior coroner is not to decide that a hearing is unnecessary unless—

(a) the coroner has invited representations from each interested person known to the coroner,

(b) no interested person has represented on reasonable grounds that a hearing should take place,

(c) it appears to the coroner that there is no real prospect of disagreement among interested persons as to the determinations or findings that the inquest could or should make, and

(d) it appears to the coroner that no public interest would be served by a hearing."

The requirements for the Coroner to be able to hold an inquest in writing are, therefore:

- invite representations from each interested person;
- have no-one represent on reasonable grounds that a hearing should take place;
- consider that there is no real prospect of disagreement as to the inquest's determinations or findings;
- and consider that no public interest would be served by a hearing.

The Chief Coroner has issued Guidance No.29 *Inquests in Writing* to assist with the interpretation of section 9C. At paragraphs 4 to 6 of that Guidance:

"4. Rule 23 allows written evidence to be admissible at an inquest hearing, if certain conditions are met.

5. Applying rule 23, coroners can conduct an inquest hearing in a courtroom[iii] by admitting written evidence, summarising that evidence sufficiently to come to a reasoned decision, and after closing the inquest, informing the interested persons of the determination, findings and conclusion in writing. In suitable cases, coroners have therefore been able to conduct documentary hearings before the new provisions on inquests in writing came into effect.

> *6. Section 9C Coroners and Justice Act 2009 ('CJA') creates a new power for coroners to decide that an inquest will be held in writing. When conducting an inquest in writing under s9C, coroners will need to open the inquest in the usual way, but then no further hearing will be required.*"

Guidance No.29 does also give us examples of the types of inquests which could be held entirely in writing at paragraph 9 (also referred to as 'Rule 23 inquests'):

- Industrial disease cases with an in-life histological diagnosis with clear work history;
- Straightforward drugs deaths with no reason to suspect suicide and no concerns surrounding the role of addiction services or healthcare provision;
- Cases where the medical cause of death remains unascertained, but there is no reason to suspect an unnatural cause or a death in state detention;
- Suicides in the community where the events are clear and no actions of a third party have given rise to concern.

The Guidance tells us the process leading up to the inquest if the coroner decides that an inquest may be suitable (paras 10 to 18):

1. Coroner should open tine inquest in the usual way;
2. Having opened the inquest, the Coroner should adjourn it pending consideration of the form the inquest should take;
3. The coroner should notify the interested persons that the coroner is considering holding an inquest in writing, on the basis that there appears to be no real prospect of disagreement as to the determination, findings or conclusion that the inquest should

make. The coroner should tell the IPs that if they are not content for the inquest to be held in writing, they need to write to the coroner requesting a hearing and explaining why one is needed;

4. When giving the interested persons this information, in order to enable them to consider whether they should make representations seeking a hearing, coroners should provide them with a copy of any document relevant to the inquest that would be disclosed to them under rule 13 (see the chapter on evidence at Chapter 8);

5. Coroners are not required to, but may decide to, notify the interested persons of the determination, findings and conclusion they anticipate reaching at the inquest so as to check whether there is any disagreement. In doing this, they should make clear that any views they express at that stage are provisional;

6. Any discussions between the coroner's officers and interested persons about the form of the inquest should be accurately recorded;

7. If the coroner decides to proceed with an inquest in writing, the interested persons should be informed of that decision;

8. In order to satisfy the requirement for open justice, basic information about the inquest in writing should be published in advance, where possible, at least seven days before the inquest is conducted. No place, date or time needs to be provided but it will mean that members of the public and press can find out that the inquest will be taking place in writing and make representations and/or request copies of documents;

9. If the coroner ultimately decides in a particular case that there should be a hearing rather than an inquest in writing, the coroner may consider whether there is any evidence that could be admitted in writing under Rule 23 of the 2013 Inquests Rules.

In terms of the inquest itself, a coroner does not have to be in court when conducting an inquest in writing. There are no additional requirements, according to the Guidance, relating to the format of the coroner's determination, findings and conclusion by virtue of it being in writing.

In reaching their decision, the coroner must follow the same process as they do when conducting an inquest via hearing. This is a three-stage process:

1. Make findings of fact based on the evidence;

2. Distil from the findings of fact 'how' the deceased came by his / her death and record this in Box 3 of the Record of Inquest;

3. State the conclusion and record this in Box 4 of the Record of Inquest.

Once the inquest has been closed, the IPs should be informed in writing of the coroner's determination, findings and conclusion, and the family should be told how to obtain a copy of the death certificate.

Finally, Guidance No.29 provides an example of a possible ruling in an inquest in writing:

> "[*Insert Heading*]
>
> *The Interested Persons are: [provide details]*
>
> *[The Interested Persons are in agreement] OR [Having received no representations on reasonable grounds that a hearing should take place, I have decided] that the Inquest into the death of [deceased's name] can be concluded under s9C Coroners and Justice Act 2009.*
>
> *[Deceased's name] was identified as confirmed by [insert details, e.g. an identity statement of [name] dated [date]]*
>
> *I have had regard to: [insert details of evidence considered, e.g. a post mortem report of [name] dated [date], Statements of [names] etc].*

I make the following findings of fact: [insert details].

Based upon those facts, I make the determination, findings and conclusion set out in the Record of Inquest attached.

[I would like to express condolences to [deceased's name]'s family.]

[Signed and dated]

Copied to the Interested Persons"

CHAPTER TEN

STARTING THE INQUEST HEARING

At the start of the inquest hearing you may:

- Argue any preliminary matters;
- Select a jury (if there is a jury);
- Hear an opening statement read by the Coroner, setting out the facts which are not in dispute;
- Hear pen-portraits from the family.

Alternatively, the Coroner may proceed directly to the evidence by way of live witnesses and witnesses read by virtue of Rule 23 of the 2013 Inquest Rules.

There is not a great deal more to say about the further arguing of preliminary matters or the Coroner's opening statement.

Below we will consider further, though: a) procedure for selecting a jury and b) pen-portraits.

SELECTION OF A JURY

Section 8 of the Coroners and Justice Act 2009 governs assembling a jury:

> "***8 Assembling a jury***
>
> *(1) The jury at an inquest (where there is a jury) is to consist of seven, eight, nine, ten or eleven persons.*

(2) For the purpose of summoning a jury, a senior coroner may summon persons (whether within or without the coroner area for which that coroner is appointed) to attend at the time and place stated in the summons.

(3) Once assembled, the members of a jury are to be sworn by or before the coroner to inquire into the death of the deceased and to give a true determination according to the evidence.

(4) Only a person who is qualified to serve as a juror in the Crown Court, the High Court and the [county court]1 , under section 1 of the Juries Act 1974 (c. 23), is qualified to serve as a juror at an inquest.

(5) The senior coroner may put to a person summoned under this section any questions that appear necessary to establish whether or not the person is qualified to serve as a juror at an inquest."

Part 5 of the 2013 Inquest Rules sets out procedures in relation to the summoning of jurors, as well as the following at Rules 32 and 33:

"***32. Validity of proceedings where jury not present***

Where an inquest hearing begins without a jury but a jury is subsequently summoned, the validity of anything done by the coroner before the jury was summoned is still effective."

"***33. Summing up and directions to the jury***

Where the coroner sits with a jury, the coroner must direct the jury as to the law and provide the jury with a summary of the evidence."

So a jury may consist of as few a seven or as many as 11 people.

For the purposes of empanelling a jury, a senior coroner may summon persons to attend, who may come from within or without the coroner's area.

In Schedule to the 2013 Inquest Rules is Form 1, used to summon jurors, and which explains a number of rules about the jurors. Key points to note are:

- A person is qualified as a juror if they are between 18 and 70 years of age, are on the electoral roll, have lived in the UK, Channel Island or Isle of Man for at least five years since turning 13 years of age and do not fall within one of the exceptions set out in Parts I and II of Schedule I to the Juries Act 1974;

- A person who qualifies as a juror is nevertheless entitled to be excused if they: a) are a full-time serving member of the navy, military or air forces and commanding officer certifies that it would be prejudicial to the efficiency of the service if they were required to be absent; b) are a coroner within the same coroner area; or c) are otherwise excused from attending;

- In relation to the discretion of the coroner, that may be exercised on the grounds of the potential juror's poor health, illness, physical disability, insufficient understanding of English, holiday arrangements or any other good reason;

- Even if the juror does not request to be excused in advance, if they attend as a juror and there is doubt as to their capability to be on the jury due to physical disability or insufficient understanding of English then they may be discharged.

Once the jury is assembled, the members are sworn by or before the coroner to inquire into the death of the deceased and to give a true determination according to the evidence.

Given that a jury can be anywhere between 7 and 11 members, it makes sense for the coroner in long inquests in particular to aim to swear in 11 jurors to ensure the inquest is not derailed should one or two suffer unexpected setbacks and need to be discharged during the course of the inquest hearing.

Under section 8(5) of the 2009 Act (see above), the coroner may put to a potential juror any question as seems necessary to establish whether or not that person is qualified to serve as a juror at the inquest. A coroner may wish to do this by providing the potential jurors a list of questions. Those questions may well be canvassed with the advocates representing the interested persons before they are provided to the jury. Examples could be:

- Whether the potential juror knew the deceased;
- Whether the potential juror knew any of those who will be witnesses at the inquest (accompanied by a list of names);
- Whether the potential juror lives or has close connection to the area in which a death occurred;
- In cases where conduct of police may be criticised, whether the potential juror has worked, or has family or close friends who have worked, in that police force;
- In cases where the conduct of a particular NHS Trust may be criticised, whether the potential juror has worked, or has family or close friends who have worked, for that NHS Trust.

Those examples are neither exhaustive nor rigid; they will of course be entirely dependent on the case itself. They will generally be chosen to ensure that the juror comes to the case with fresh eyes and no pre-existing bias in one direction or another. Do bear in mind that questions as to physical disability, understanding of English, illness and the like will have been posed already in Form 1 when that reached the potential juror as part of their summons.

PEN PORTRAITS

'Pen portraits' are relatively unique in legal proceedings, in that they of themselves have little to no evidential value. However, they can be an important part of the process for the bereaved family and, indeed, for reminding all present of the person (or persons) at the heart of the process.

A pen portrait is something which enables the bereaved family to tell the court about their deceased loved one. It often takes the form of a statement read out in open court by a family member, and may be accompanied by photographs. There is no set structure for the portrait, nor 'checklist' of things which may be included. The family may wish to say only a few words in tribute, or they may wish to read a long statement covering their loved one's interests, hobbies and personality. Of course, the family may also wish to say nothing at all, preferring to keep their feelings private.

The Chief Coroner has endorsed the use of pen portraits in inquests where the family are present, whether the proceedings are short and informal or longer affairs with a jury and several advocates. Whilst there is no set structure of a pen portrait, the Chief Coroner has set out guidance to assist in understanding those contemplating their use, at Guidance No.41.

At paragraph 4 of the Guidance, the Chief Coroner sets out the different forms an inquest may take, with guidance as to how pen portrait material fits into that:

1. An inquest entirely in writing held under Rule 23 of the 2013 Inquest Rules – pen portraits do not usually arise in these inquests because it is just the coroner in the courtroom and no family members are present;

2. Inquests where only the coroner and family members are present – this is normally an intimate hearing, which can be fairly

informal and relaxed. The family might tell the coroner something about their loved one in this sort of hearing;

3. Coroner sitting along without a jury but with interested persons present (with or without advocates) – the Chief Coroner expects a coroner sitting without a jury to adopt a relaxed and flexible approach to the admission of pen portrait material. It will be incumbent on the coroner to determine what is permissible for the family to adduce, and when is appropriate;

4. Coroner sitting with a jury – in inquests heard by a coroner and a jury, photographs and other imagery of the circumstances of the death may well form part of the evidence placed before the court. In such circumstances, families may well wish to include some photographs or imagery from the life of the deceased. The type of material to be permitted, the amount and its timing is a matter of judgment for the coroner. It may therefore be sensible for the coroner to seek disclosure from the family of the material they wish to adduce by way of pen portrait, and directions at the pre-inquest review stage should cater for this.

CHAPTER ELEVEN

WITNESSES

With all the preliminary matters out of the way, the jury sworn (if there is to be a jury), a summary of undisputed facts by the coroner and any pen portraits having been read, the inquest will turn to hearing witness evidence.

Witness evidence can be a combination of live and written evidence. We have covered the provisions relating to written evidence in some detail in the previous chapter, so the focus of this chapter will be the evidence of live witnesses.

As a preliminary point, the order in which witnesses are called is a matter for the coroner. Ideally, participants in the inquest will have received a timetable in advance setting out the order of witnesses. The coroner is not obliged by law to produce an advance witness list, but it is regarded as good practice (*R v HM Coroner for Lincoln, ex parte Hay* (2000) Inquest LR 1).

The coroner has wide discretion to decide which witnesses will be called, as made clear in *R (Mack) v HM Coroner for Birmingham & Solihull* (2011) EWCA Civ 712 at paragraph 9:

> "*9. There is clear authority and it is not in dispute that [the statute] gives to the coroner a wide discretion – or perhaps more appropriately a wide area of judgment — whom it is expedient to call. The court will only intervene if satisfied that the decision made was one which was not properly open to him on Wednesbury principles.*"

Notwithstanding that wide discretion, the coroner is required to call sufficient witnesses to undertake a proper inquiry into the relevant issues. *R (Ahmed) v HM Coroner for South & East Cumbria* (2009) EWHC 1653 (Admin) held at paragraph 35:

> "*35. It is also common ground that a Coroner is under a duty to call sufficient evidence to enable him or her to answer the questions set out in Rule 36 [of the Coroners Rules 1984]. The Coroner is not required to call each and every witness who might be able to give some relevant evidence on any possible aspect of an inquiry. I will look in due course more closely at the law affecting disclosure of material before an inquest or in association with it.*"

LIVE WITNESSES

When a live witness is called, the Coroner will lead the questioning of that witness (Rule 21 of the 2013 Inquest Rules). They will ask the questions first and, in practice, may well cover the vast majority of the anticipated evidence.

Under rule 19(1) of the 2013 Inquests Rules a coroner must allow any interested person who so requests to examine any witness, either in person or through their representative.

When questioning on behalf of the interested person, the advocate will generally find themselves stopped by the coroner if they are asking any question that is a) merely repeating questioning that has been aired by the coroner (or others) already; or b) asking questions the coroner considers to be irrelevant (as to the latter, see Rule 19(2) of the 2013 Inquests Rules). In practice, then, it is not unusual for the advocate to find that they have very few questions to ask of a witness, if any at all. This is particularly so if they are one of the last of a long line of advocates.

The witness is protected from self-incrimination. Rule 22 of the 2013 Inquests Rules provides as follows:

> "***22.— Self incrimination***
>
> *(1) No witness at an inquest is obliged to answer any question tending to incriminate him or her.*

(2) Where it appears to the coroner that a witness has been asked such a question, the coroner must inform the witness that he or she may refuse to answer it."

By virtue of Rule 21 of the 2013 Inquest Rules, the advocate whose witness it is will ask questions last; so if that advocate's client is also a witness, for example, they will be the last to ask questions. Once the coroner has concluded his or her questioning, any other interested person who wishes to question the witness will be invited to do so. In practice, the family (or their representative) is often invited to ask questions after the coroner. The order thereafter is a matter for the coroner. To be clear, generally speaking the coroner tends to ask each advocate in turn whether they have questions for that witness once the coroner and family are finished, rather than requiring them to indicate in advance whether they wish to ask questions, as one reading of the rule might suggest.

Finally, if there is a jury they will be asked by the coroner whether they have any questions. They do not stand up and ask questions orally; they will write the question down and pass it to the coroner. The coroner then ensures the relevance of the question before asking it of the witness him or herself.

As an advocate who may be used to criminal or civil proceedings, one key thing to remember is that when questioning the witness you are not cross-examining that witness. The inquest is still very much considered an inquisitorial process, rather than the sort of adversarial process into which fits criminal or civil proceedings. In practice, of course, the advocates will be concerned with ensuring that they protect their own client's positions. Therefore, whilst the advocate will not be 'putting their case' or asking sharp, short, closed questions in the way they might in other jurisdictions, they will nevertheless be ensuring that they lay the foundations for closing arguments aimed at insulating their clients from direct or indirect criticism.

This is a more important role than may at first be thought. Whilst the inquest proceedings themselves cannot apportion civil or criminal liability, there is nothing to stop other processes flowing from the findings of the inquest. For example, the 2016 Hillsborough Inquest 'unlawful killing' conclusion paved the way to the prosecution of the former Chief Superintendant David Duckenfield.

For those representing the family, they may therefore not only be seeking to expose all the facts behind their loved one's death, but to ascertain whether there are grounds for a civil claim against any party, or indeed grounds to persuade the Crown Prosecution Service to consider a criminal prosecution.

RELEVANT CASES

R (on the application of Al-Fayed) v Assistant Deputy Coroner of Inner West London (2008) EWHC 713

The case was an application for permission to apply for JR of the coroner's decision to refuse to call His Royal Highness the Duke of Edinburgh to give evidence, and to require Her Majesty the Queen to answer a number of specified questions at the inquests into the deaths of Diana, Princess of Wales and Mr Dodi Al-Fayed.

The application was rejected:

> *"19. In our judgment the Coroner was entitled to conclude that the new theory, whether it went to rumour and speculation or indeed "how" the deceased met their deaths, when examined in the light of existing evidence, did not make it expedient to ask the questions intended to be raised with the Duke of Edinburgh, and the questions asked of Her Majesty The Queen. As he put it in his judgment, the approach the Coroner had adopted at the outset had led to submissions which in effect said, "the further you have gone, the further you ought to go". The Coroner considered and addressed each of the "issues" identified by the claimant's solicitors in relation to the purpose of the Inquests. The question whether it was expedient for these purposes for any evidence (from whomsoever) to be given on these or any other issues*

was pre-eminently a matter for his judgment. His analysis of the issues in his ruling demonstrates that there was nothing in the proposed evidence which would be of advantage to the jury when reaching their verdict. The stark reality was that enough was enough.

20. The Coroner's approach was neither illogical nor unreasonable, and his conclusion was not flawed. He was required to make a judgment based on whether it was expedient in the particular context of the facts and issues relevant to these inquests. In that context he was entitled to have regard to the vast amount of evidence which had been called and the very limited evidence which remained to be called. As he put it:

> *"in keeping open the question whether it might be expedient to call the Duke of Edinburgh I was anxious to see what evidence emerged during the inquests that might alter my initial view. Looking at the whole of the evidence and keeping firmly in mind that it is for the jury and not me to decide what evidence is to be accepted or rejected, nothing has emerged to persuade me it will be expedient to call the Duke of Edinburgh … Inquiries of Her Majesty The Queen should not be made as suggested by Mr Al Fayed on the basis that they will not assist the jury to answer the statutory questions."*

21. In our judgment the contention that this court should interfere with these carefully considered decisions was unarguable. Accordingly the applications were dismissed."

<u>*R (Hair) v HM Coroner for Staffordshire* (2010) EWHC 2580 (Admin)</u>

The High Court considered various challenges to the adequacy of the inquest into the death of a prisoner who had been found unconscious with a ligature around his neck, and had subsequently died.

One of the challenges was to the decision of the coroner not to call two prison governors and a prison officer to give evidence, which was said to be relevant to (amongst other things) allegations the deceased had made of bullying by a prison governor. There was some contention around a written statement found amongst adjudication papers relating to the deceased.

In allowing the application:

> "*42. I have some sympathy for the coroner who, in common with the parties, was dealing with inexcusably late disclosure which seems to have caught everyone on the hop. Nevertheless, the responsibility for ensuring that all relevant witnesses were called was ultimately his. It seems to me that it was his duty to ensure, even at the expense of an adjournment (had that proved necessary), that all relevant witnesses were called on the question of who (if anyone) had access to the written statement and why it was apparently ignored.*
>
> *[…]*
>
> *The failure on the coroner's part to call those witnesses, or even to comment upon the significance of the documentary record, seems to me fatally to undermine the integrity of the inquest. Given also that the error was a result of late production of documents by the state, it seems to me that the state has, partly as a result of its own conduct, not been held properly to account and that the inquisition must, in those circumstances, be quashed and another inquest ordered.*"

<u>*R (Goodson) v Bedfordshire and Luton Coroner* (2004) EWHC 2931 (Admin)</u>

Following an operation, the deceased died. His daughter challenged the decision of the coroner in the inquest to refuse to call relevant medical experts.

In considering whether independent expert evidence was required, the High Court held:

> "*72. In this case it is relevant that the coroner, though experienced, was not medically qualified. Moreover the pathologist could give him only*

limited assistance in relation to the care exercised by the surgeon who performed the procedure on Mr Coleman and the care he received thereafter. On the other hand, the coroner did have the hospital notes, the GP's letter, and relevant expert evidence, albeit not independent evidence, from the surgeon herself and from the specialist senior registrar, both of whom were experienced practitioners. That evidence could be probed and was in fact subject to cross-examination by the claimant's solicitor. The coroner also had the benefit of statistical evidence (provided by the surgeon in her comments, but backed up with references to the textbooks) as to the risk of complications and mortality from this elective procedure. Further, in this case there was no expert evidence on behalf of the claimant suggesting any deficiency in the care received by the deceased or in the hospital procedures. Such suggestion as there was of negligence came only through cross-examination or submission by the claimant's solicitor.

73. The coroner himself makes clear in his written reasons that he was satisfied in the circumstances that there was no negligence and that there was no need for a "systems review" of the hospital procedures; but that had he taken a different view he would have obtained independent expert evidence and/or undertaken a systems review. There was no question of his perceiving his powers to be limited in any material respect if the matter proceeded as an ordinary inquest without also constituting an article 2 investigation. The matter therefore comes down to whether the coroner's judgment that fuller investigation was not required in the circumstances was a lawful judgment. In the context of the sufficiency of an investigation under article 2 it seems to me that the court, rather than simply asking whether the coroner's judgment was reasonably open to him in the Wednesbury sense, must form its own judgment on whether more was required, in particular by way of independent expert evidence. In forming such a judgment, however, the court must take account of its own lack of medical expertise and must pay an appropriate degree of deference to the judgment of the coroner, who is more experienced in these matters and was closer to the actual evidence in the case.

> *74. Applying that approach, and taking due account of the criticisms made by Mr Powers of the evidence that was before the coroner, I am not persuaded that the coroner was wrong to view the matter as he did.*"

R (LePage) v HM Assistant Deputy Coroner for Inner South London (2012) EWHC 1485 (Admin)

There was an issue in this case as to whether restraint and search might have contributed to the death and the family wished the coroner to call a forensic pathologist who they had instructed in order to explore the issue. The family accordingly challenged the decision of the coroner not to call this expert.

The Court concluded that the coroner did not act unlawfully in not calling the expert, but did consider that it might have been better to do so as a matter of 'practical justice':

> "*62. I stress that there was no duty to call Dr James, no requirement to do so, and the exercise of the coroner's discretion not to call him cannot be criticised. It was not unlawful to refuse to call him. But in all the circumstances it might have been better, not as a matter of law but as a matter of practical justice. As Brown LJ observed in an inquest context in R v Inner West London Coroner, ex parte Dallaglio (1994) 4 All ER 139, 155, citing Bingham LJ in a natural justice context in R v Chief Constable of the Thames Valley Police, ex parte Cotton (1990) IRLR 344, 352: 'This is a field in which appearances are generally thought to matter'.*"

CHAPTER TWELVE

CLOSING SUBMISSIONS

Once the evidence has all been called or otherwise aired before the court, the coroner invites closing submissions from interested persons (or their representatives).

Rule 27 of the 2013 Inquests Rules states:

> "*27. No address as to facts*
>
> *No person may address the coroner or the jury as to the facts of who the deceased was and how, when and where the deceased came by his or her death*".

This provision may sound alien to those practitioners who are used to the criminal or civil litigation forum. In an inquest context, neither the interested person nor their advocate may seek to persuade the coroner or the jury as to the way they should interpret the facts in reaching their conclusions.

Their submissions instead focus on which conclusions should be left to the coroner (or the jury, if one is empanelled). To that limited extent only, advocates may find themselves making reference to the facts. This may well be a key part of the process for certain advocates, who wish to persuade the coroner against leaving conclusions for consideration which could impact upon their client. For example, the advocate may wish to persuade the coroner that they should not (or, legally, cannot) leave a conclusion of unlawful killing to themselves / the jury. Conversely, the advocate representing the family may wish to argue that such a conclusion can be left for the coroner / jury's consideration.

To what standard do the advocates turn when seeking to persuade the coroner at this stage? The answer is helpfully set out in Chief Coroners Law Sheet No.2: 'Galbraith Plus'.

Those practitioners with a criminal law background will be familiar with the concept of 'Galbraith'. The criminal case of *R v Galbraith [1981]* 1 WLR 1039 set out the seminal criminal legal test when determining whether the prosecution have produced evidence sufficient to leave a case for the defence to answer (if the answer is 'no' then the Judge will stop the case and decline to even leave it to the jury).

Under *Galbraith* A judge must stop the case where <u>either:</u>

1. There is no evidence that the crime alleged has been committed by the defendant; <u>or</u>

2. The evidence is of such a tenuous character (such as by virtue of its inherent weakness or vagueness) that taken at its highest a jury properly directed could not properly convict.

The coronial system has borrowed and adapted this test in determining whether a conclusion should be left to the coroner (or the jury, if one is empanelled). As a result, inquest law relies upon a test called '*Galbraith Plus*'.

In Chief Coroner's Law Sheet No.2:

> "*2. In the criminal law the test is laid down in the well-known case of R v Galbraith. In short the test is that a case should not be left to the jury where there is no or no sufficient evidence. Borderline cases can safely be left to the discretion of the judge.*
>
> *3. But there is now authority in coroner law that suggests that the test is more than just the Galbraith test. It has been described as Galbraith plus.*

4. In R (Secretary of State for Justice) v HM Deputy Coroner for the Eastern District of West Yorkshire (2012) EWHC 1623 (Admin) Haddon-Cave J ruled that the Galbraith test alone was not enough. More was needed:

> *'It is clear, therefore, that when coroners are deciding whether or not to leave a particular verdict to a jury, they should apply a dual test comprising both limbs or 'schools of thought' [as discussed in Galbraith], i.e. coroners should (a) ask the classic pure Galbraith question "Is there evidence on which a jury properly directed could properly convict etc.?" … plus (b) also ask the question "Would it be **safe** for the jury to convict on the evidence before it?' [emphasis added]*

*5. The coroner must therefore first be satisfied that there is enough evidence, in the former Galbraith sense that there is sufficient evidence upon which a jury properly directed could properly reach a particular conclusion. In addition (described in the West Yorkshire case as the 'modest gloss or addition') the coroner must also be satisfied that it is **safe** to leave the conlusion to the jury: ibid, paras 17-25. The two questions for the coroner therefore are: Is there enough evidence to leave this conclusion to the jury? And, if so, would it be safe on the evidence for the jury to reach this conclusion? Failure to ask and answer either question may render the conclusion vulnerable to challenge by way of judicial review (as in the West Yorkshire case)."*

Therefore, the advocate seeking to persuade the coroner that they should not leave (for example) a conclusion of unlawful killing to themselves / the jury will refer to the evidence only so far as they consider is needed to:

a) Argue that there is no evidence upon which a jury / the coroner properly directed could reach that conclusion; OR

b) Argue that if there is such evidence it is of such a tenuous character that no jury/coroner properly directed could reach that conclusion; OR

c) If there is such evidence and it is more than merely tenuous, it would nevertheless not be safe for the jury/coroner to reach that conclusion.

Conversely, the advocate arguing that a coroner / jury should be permitted to consider a certain conclusion will be arguing that there is evidence to support the conclusion, it is of more than a tenuous nature and it would be safe for a jury/coroner properly directed to reach that conclusion.

The 'plus' limb of *Galbraith plus* may not be as easy to understand on its face; after all, what is meant by it being 'safe' to leave a conclusion to the coroner/jury? The Law Sheet does address this in paragraphs 9 to 12:

> "*9. The word 'safe' is not defined or explained. It should therefore be given its ordinary English meaning, the coroner exercising his or her own discretion judicially on a case by case basis. 'Safe' may have originated from the Court of Appeal's jurisdiction in criminal cases in its negative form of 'unsafe'10 (originally 'unsafe or unsatisfactory'), but consideration of 'lurking doubt' or similar postconviction cases will not help in this context.*
>
> *10. Lord Woolf MR had adopted a similar approach, but not using the word 'safe', in the familiar case of R v Inner South London Coroner, ex parte Douglas-Williams [1999] 1 All ER 344, based upon the coroner's role being more inquisitorial and therefore having, at least indirectly, a greater say as to what verdict/conclusion the jury should consider than a judge at an adversarial trial. He stated at 349:*
>
> > *'If it appears there are circumstances which, in a particular situation, mean in the judgment of the coroner, acting reasonably and fairly,* ***it is not in the interest of justice that a particular verdict should be left to the jury****, he need not leave*

> *that verdict. He, for example, need not leave all possible verdicts just because there is technically evidence to support them. It is sufficient if he leaves those verdicts which realistically reflect the thrust of the evidence as a whole. To leave all possible verdicts could in some situations merely confuse and overburden the jury and if that is the coroner's conclusion he cannot be criticised if he does not leave a particular verdict.' [emphasis added]*

11.Lord Woolf did, however, use the word 'safe' in an even earlier case, R v HM Coroner for Exeter and East Devon ex parte Palmer. Having described the duty of the coroner as 'a filter to avoid injustice' he stated:

> *'In a difficult case, the Coroner is carrying out an evaluation exercise. He is looking at the evidence before him as a whole and saying to himself, without deciding matters which are the province of the jury, 'Is this a case where it would be* ***safe*** *for the jury to come to the conclusion that there had been an unlawful killing?' If he reaches the conclusion that, because the evidence is so inherently weak, vague or inconsistent with other evidence, it would not be safe for a jury to come to the verdict, then he has to withdraw the issue from the jury.' [emphasis added]*

12. In R (Longfield Care Homes Ltd) v HM Coroner for Blackburn Mitting J described the coroner's two-stage exercise as (1) a matter of judgment in deciding whether there is sufficient evidence, and (2) if there is, a matter of 'discretion in an appropriate case, and when ***the interests of justice*** *require it, not to leave a verdict/conclusion to the jury, even though on the Galbraith test there is evidence to support it'. [emphasis added]"*

RELEVANT CASES

R (on the application of Police Officer B50) v HM Assistant Coroner for East Yorkshire and Kingston Upon Hull [2023] EWHC 81 (Admin)

This was a case where the claimant, a police officer, challenged the decision of a coroner to leave the issue of unlawful killing to the inquest jury. The Divisional Court dismissed the application but considered the utility of the '*Galbraith plus*' test in so doing. At paragraphs 64 to 65, having considered various decisions setting out the basis for the *Galbraith plus* test:

> "*64. As this review of the authorities shows, it is established by authority that is binding upon us that there is some (if small) distinction between the position of a coroner deciding what verdict to leave to a jury after hearing all the evidence and of a judge considering whether to stop a case after the conclusion of the prosecution case. The distinction flows from the differences in process between the two jurisdictions, as explained by Lord Woolf in Douglas-Williams at 348-349 and Collins J in Anderson at [21]-[22]: see [41] and [44] above. Although the Court of Appeal has identified considerations of safety as relevant to the coroner's decision, there is limited guidance from the Court of Appeal about what should inform those considerations. Though he used the word "safe" at [46] of Palmer Lord Woolf MR provided no guidance in Palmer ; and such guidance as he gave in Douglas-Williams suggested that questions of safety would involve considerations that were not directly related to the sufficiency of the evidence: see the italicised passage set out at [41] above. We reiterate that in Galbraith itself Lord Lane emphasised that "safe" and "unsafe" can mean sufficiency or insufficiency of evidence on which a jury could properly reach a guilty verdict. In contrast, Bennett suggests that the concept of safety is an evidential one: see [54] above. This seems to us to be in accordance with conventional principle and, in almost all cases, to provide the answer to Leveson J's rhetorical question: on the face of it, if a verdict is (properly) open to the (properly directed) jury*

on the evidence how can it be said to be in the interests of justice that it not be left for the jury to consider? Any other approach, save for one based upon the wider interests of justice as suggested in Douglas-Williams runs straight into the risk of usurping the proper function of the jury. This risk is, to our minds, accentuated in the light of Maughan now that all short form conclusions, including suicide and unlawful killing, may now be reached on the balance of probabilities: see the Chief Coroner's Leeming Lecture delivered on 22 July 2022, at paragraph 51.

65. We are not strictly bound by other first instance decisions, but should follow them unless convinced that they are wrong. We doubt whether we would have formalised the " Galbraith plus" test as was done in the West Yorkshire case; but it has been endorsed by subsequent first instance decisions even though the parameters of the "plus" element have not been made clear. We are not convinced that the formulation is wrong; but the devil is in the detail of what may render it unsafe to leave a conclusion to the jury in a case where, without usurping the function of the jury, it appears that there is evidence sufficient to enable a properly directed jury properly to return that conclusion. What is clear is that it is not open to a coroner, in a case which passes the classic Galbraith test of evidential sufficiency, to withdraw a conclusion under the guise of lack of "safety" just because they might not agree with a particular outcome, however strongly. While being fully alert to the need for the coroner (and the court) to act as a filter to avoid injustice, we agree with the observation of Pepperall J that "where there is evidence upon which a jury properly directed could properly reach a particular conclusion or finding then it is likely to follow that the jury could safely reach such conclusion or finding." Likely but not inevitable; and, on present authority, it appears that the categories of consideration that could (at least in theory) render it unsafe to leave a suitably evidenced conclusion to the jury are not closed."

R (Hair) v HM Coroner for Staffordshire South (2010) EWHC 2850 (Admin)

This was an Article 2 inquest into the death of a person who had hung himself whilst in custody. As part of this application, the High Court considered the argument that Rule 40 of the Coroner's Rules 1984 (the equivalent provision to Rule 27 of the 2013 Inquests Rules) prevented the jury reaching a proper conclusion on key issues of fact and so was incompatible with Article 2 of the European Convention on Human Rights. That part of the application was rejected as follows:

> "*47. The requirement under Article 2 is to ensure that the state is held properly to account in respect of any death for which it may be responsible. Sadly, that typically embraces the death of prisoners in custody. No particular form of procedure is required, however, so long as there is an effective investigation, in which the family of the deceased person is involved. Addressing the coroner or jury as to facts is not, in my judgment, an essential pre-requisite of an effective investigation.*
>
> *48. Miss Gerry points in this case to the difficulties she laboured under when addressing the coroner as to the questions that should be put to the jury. Nonetheless, the questions that were put corresponded to what she and all other Counsel involved wanted to be put. She was also allowed to address the coroner, as were the other Counsel involved, in reminding him as to what the evidence was as to who had access to the adjudication papers and the written statement. To the extent that the coroner's summing-up to the jury was deficient, she can complain of that without recourse to Rule 40. To the extent that it was adequate, she can have no complaint. An inability to address the coroner as to the facts generally does not make an adequate summing-up inadequate.*
>
> *49. Miss Gerry seeks an order quashing Rule 40 on the grounds of incompatibility with Article 2 of ECHR . I decline such an order. I do not consider Rule 40 to be incompatible with Article 2. As I have said, no particular process is required to hold the state to account, as long as it is effective. Miss Gerry's submission, if accepted, would open the door*

to lengthy submissions in all cases having any state involvement. I do not consider this to be an essential element of what is in many respects an inquisitorial process, notwithstanding that there are also adversarial elements. Rule 40 has been around for a long time, and, whilst it has attracted comment, no-one has suggested that it is invalid and Middleton supports the proposition that the Coroner's Rules are, in general terms, ECHR-compatible.

50. Alternatively, Miss Gerry asks that Rule 40 be read so as to allow interested parties to address the coroner as to facts where necessary to ensure Article 2 obligations are complied with. Tempting though it is to accede to this submission, I decline to do so. Ultimately, the resolution of this sort of case turns not on what submissions as to facts the parties are allowed to advance, but on the adequacy of the coronial process. Had the coroner in this case called all relevant evidence and given an impeccable summing-up, there would be no scope for complaint simply on account of the absence of the opportunity to make submissions as to the facts. As it happens, I have found deficiencies in the coronial process in the instant case, but the criticism of Rule 40 adds nothing. In my judgment, the ability to make submissions as to the facts, whether to the coroner or the jury, is not necessary to ensure compliance with Article 2. That being so, the suggested construction of Rule 40 is inappropriate."

CHAPTER THIRTEEN

CLOSING OF THE INQUEST AND CONCLUSIONS

Following the closing submissions of the advocates, the coroner will either retire to consider their final conclusions or will sum-up the case to the jury, and direct them as to the law.

The final decisions of the coroner/jury are to be recorded by completing the Record of Inquest. A copy of this can be found in the Schedule to the 2013 Inquests Rules, and in the Annex to this book.

Box 1 of the Record of Inquest is where the coroner/jury records the name of the deceased.

Box 2 is where the medical cause of death is recorded.

Box 3 is where the coroner/jury records answers to the questions how, when and where (and, for Article 2 inquests, in what circumstances) the deceased came about their death.

Box 4 records the conclusion of the coroner/jury as to the death.

This section of the book will focus on sections 3 and 4 with a focus as to 'how' the deceased came by their death. This is likely to be the area of the inquest to which the vast majority of the evidence is directed – and certainly the contentious evidence.

The Chief Coroner has issued guidance to assist with this particular subject: Chief Coroner's Guidance No.17: *conclusions, short-form and narrative.*

THREE-STAGE PROCESS TO REACHING A CONCLUSION

When the coroner/jury reaches boxes 3 and 4 of the Record of Inquest, Chief Coroner's Guidance No.17 sets out a three-stage process that should be followed (paragraph 8).

1. To make findings of fact based upon the evidence. When a coroner sits alone, the key findings of fact should be stated orally in open court – but not written on the Record of Inquest. Where there is a jury, they need to be directed to make findings of fact for themselves based upon the evidence they have heard. They will not normally record these findings of fact publicly except insofar as they form part of the answer to boxes 3 or 4.

2. To distil from the findings of fact 'how' the deceased came by their death and to record that briefly in Box 3. It is clear from this that Box 3 does not require a comprehensive or complex response to the question of 'how' the deceased came by their death. The Guidance, in fact, states: "*Normally, the answer to 'how' will be a brief one sentence summary taken from the findings of fact in (1) above.*"

3. To record the conclusion, which must flow from and be consistent with (1) and (2) above, in Box 4.

BOX THREE: 'HOW' THE DECEASED CAME BY THEIR DEATH

As noted above, the Guidance makes clear that box three does not require the sort of detailed explanation which the casual reader of the form may be forgiven for thinking it does.

At paragraph 8, the Guidance provides the following examples of 'how' in Box 3:

- 'By hanging from an exposed beam using a ligature made from a bedsheet';
- 'By drowning while swimming from his small fishing boat in the open sea';
- 'From injuries caused in a motor collision while a backseat passenger in her father's car';
- 'From trauma consistent with an un-witnessed fall downstairs';
- 'By exposure to asbestos fibres during the course of his occupation as a plumber'.

The Guidance adds: "*To these words will be added the date and place of death where known and, where necessary, any further words which briefly explain how the deceased came by his/her death*".

BOX FOUR: CONCLUSIONS

Box four is where the coroner/jury records their formal conclusion as to 'how' the deceased came by their death.

There are two alternative types of conclusion:

1. A short-form conclusion. This is a word or a phrase (e.g. 'suicide' 'unlawful killing') which encapsulates the cause of the person's death;
2. A narrative conclusion. As the name suggests, this will be a section of narrative which sets out the coroner/jury's view as to the cause of death and may, accordingly, encompass a number of causes.

Whilst these are described as 'alternatives' in the Guidance, they can also be combined.

SHORT-FORM CONCLUSIONS

The notes to the Record of Inquest contain the following non-exhaustive list of short-form conclusions:

- Accident or misadventure;
- Alcohol/drug related;
- Industrial disease;
- Lawful or unlawful killing;
- Natural causes;
- Open conclusion;
- Road traffic collision;
- Stillbirth;
- Suicide.

Paragraph 16 of the Guidance refers the reader to this list and adds "*The list is not exclusive, but straying from the list will usually be unwise*".

The standard of proof for reaching any of these conclusions is the civil standard – i.e. the balance of probabilities. This means that the jury/coroner must find that it is more likely than not that this is how the deceased came by their death.

Up until 2020, the standard of proof for unlawful killing and suicide was the criminal standard (i.e. so that the jury / coroner was 'sure' – also known as 'beyond reasonable doubt'). However, the Supreme Court reversed that long-standing position in the case of *R (on the application of Maughan) v HM Senior Coroner for Oxfordshire* (2020) UKSC 46, holding that all conclusions would be considered against the civil standard.

'Neglect' is not listed on the Record of Inquest, for good reason: it is not a conclusion in itself, but it can be a finding recorded as part of the conclusion in Box 4. For example 'natural causes contributed to by neglect'. Just because it is not a conclusion in itself, it does not follow that the coroner need not be satisfied that neglect can be considered on *Galbraith plus* principles. Those principles still apply (see chapter 12).

NARRATIVE CONCLUSIONS

The Guidance assists in relation to narrative conclusions, at paragraphs 21 to 31. At paragraphs 25 to 30:

> "*25. The higher courts have repeatedly emphasised the need for brevity in a narrative conclusion. A sentence or two, or a single short paragraph, will be sufficient. Longer narrative conclusions are neither clear nor accessible and should not be given.*
>
> *26. Narrative conclusions are not to be confused with findings of fact in the three-stage process. If the three-stage process is properly followed, there will often be no need for a narrative conclusion.*
>
> *27. In general, a narrative conclusion should be used only where the three-stage process (culminating in a short-form conclusion) is insufficient. For example, a short-form conclusion may be insufficient where the jury would wish to express a conclusion in a prison death case on a major issue such as procedures leading to two persons sharing a cell together. [xi]*
>
> *28. Narrative conclusions must be directed to the issues which are central to the cause of death. The coroner does not have to state a conclusion on every issue raised. [xii]*

> *29. Where a jury is invited to write a narrative, the coroner will usually identify the issues or areas of fact which the jury needs to address, guiding them with examples of possible narrative conclusions.*
>
> *30. Alternatively, the coroner may choose to provide the jury with written questions in the form of a questionnaire. In such cases, the questions and answers will stand as the narrative conclusion. They will become part of the Record of Inquest and will be read out in public. Questionnaires should not be lengthy."*

SPECIFIC SHORT-FORM CONCLUSIONS

ACCIDENT OR MISADVENTURE

There has been some suggestion that 'accident' and 'misadventure' are two separate concepts in coronial law: the first denoting something over which there is no human control, and the second denoting some deliberate (albeit lawful) human act which has taken an unexpected turn leading to death.

The Courts have not generally supported such a delineation, and the two conclusions continue to appear together in the short-form conclusion list in the Record of Inquest.

In *R v Portsmouth Coroner, ex parte Anderson* (1987) 1 WLR 1640 the Cort considered the differences (or otherwise) between 'accident' and 'misadventure'. At 1646, *per* Mann J:

> "*Thurston's, The Law and Practice on Coroners, 3rd ed. (1985), p. 145, contains this passage under the rubric 'Accident and misadventure':*
>
> > *'To a large extent the distinction between accident and misadventure is a matter of semantics and the two are often used interchangeably. It is submitted that a verdict of accident is the appropriate verdict to return when the death is caused by an occurrence which could not have been foreseen, whereas*

> *misadventure should be reserved for those circumstances when the death occurred as the result of a lawful or unlawful intentional human act unforseeably leading to death.'*

The distinction is indeed sophisticated, if distinction there be, and it is a distinction drawn where in the ordinary meaning of language, in my judgment, no distinction is to be found. It is distinction which seems to me to be without purpose or effect and, on any view, it lacks consequence. Coroners and their Juries would be relieved of an unnecessary burden and verdicts on deaths occurring in similar circumstances could become consistent if the contrast between 'accident' and 'misadventure' is eliminated from consideration. In my judgment, "accident" is all that is requisite and the word 'misadventure' which had an apparent vogue in 1887 should now be given its quietus as signifying some contrast with 'accident.'"

Similarly, in *R(Benton) v HM Coroner for Birmingham and Solihull* (1998) 162 JP 807 the Court considered the conclusion of 'accident or misadventure':

"*The Applicant refers to the definition of misadventure in Jervis on Coroners (11th Ed.). At paragraph 13-24 which reads:*

> *'No distinction is drawn between accident and misadventure in the conclusion. It is sometimes suggested that 'accident' connotes something over which there is no human control, or an unintended act, while 'misadventure' indicates some deliberate (but lawful) human act which has unexpectedly taken a turn that leads to death. Even if this distinction exists in logic, it is clear that coroners have not observed it in practice, and accordingly, for statistical purposes, these conclusions are treated as being the same. The Divisional Court has encouraged this trend, treating the distinction between accident and misadventure as 'without purpose and effect,' and suggesting the suppression of the latter in favour of the former. It is thus necessary to explain to the jury that 'accident' can mean the*

> *unexpected result of a deliberate act, and that recording such conclusion does not deprive any person of any civil remedy he may otherwise have.'*

Clearly this passage does represent the law on this matter ..."

The settled view of the Courts, then, seems to be that in reality there is little, if any, signficiant distinction between 'accident' and 'misadventure'. Unless and until there is a judgment which seeks to change this position, the two remain conjoined in the list of possible conclusions which a coroner or jury may reach.

R v Her Majesty's Coroner for Northamptonshire (Kettering District) (1995) 10 WLUK 221 was a fairly interesting case, where the High Court considered that a conclusion of 'accident' was not an inaccurate conclusion in relation to a man who died after ingesting ten ecstasy tablets voluntarily and then failing to receive potentially life-saving medical treatment. The Court held that the conclusion was incomplete – both parties agreed that the jury ought to have also been left with a possible conclusion of "non-dependent drug abuse" – but it was nevertheless appropriate. (*note:* 'dependent / non-dependent abuse of drugs' was the predecessor to the modern conclusion of 'drug related' which is considered below)

ALCOHOL/DRUG RELATED

The predecessor conclusion to this one was 'dependent/non-dependent abuse of drugs'. The current conclusion is arguably far more neutral. There was some concern that any stigma attached to the phrase "abuse of drugs" be avoided and, indeed, it made its way to the higher courts for that reason. Most prominently, in *R (Kendall) v Inner South London Coroner* (1988) 1 WLR 1186 the Court considered the conclusion of death by 'acute abuse of a drug' in relation to a 14-year old child. The child had died after inhaling Tippex thinning fluid. The child's mother was greatly distressed by the conclusion, due to the stigma which she felt attached to it; she wished to ensure that the conclusion made no reference to 'drugs'.

At 1191H, *per* Simon Brown LJ:

> "*As it seems to me, two central considerations should be in mind when determining the proper approach to the various forms of verdict suggested in the notes to the scheduled form of inquisition.*
>
> *The first such consideration is the application within the coroner's jurisdiction of a clearly established policy of avoiding so far as possible any unnecessary stigma to the memory of the deceased … It was doubtless this same policy which occasioned the removal from the 1984 edition of the Coroners Rules of the suggested verdict of 'chronic alcoholism': such a verdict being needlessly offensive and wounding to the memory of the deceased …*
>
> *[…]*
>
> *The other crucial consideration is the actual purpose of these various suggested forms of verdict. The primary if not indeed the sole purpose of entering a verdict of the kind here in question must surely be to alert the public to certain specific dangers. It is this desirable social end which, on occasion, outweighs the first consideration and justifies departure from the policy of not stigmatising the deceased.*
>
> *Viewed in the light of those considerations, it seems to me plain that the verdict with which we are here concerned was both unnecessarily wounding to the deceased's family and positively misleading in so far as it was designed to warn the public against the dangers of solvent abuse …*"

Simon Brown LJ went on to opine that solvent abuse deaths should not be designated as drug abuse deaths: "*In my judgment the lawful options are these. (1) accident, or just possibly misadventure. Although commentators have hitherto suggested that these verdicts carry distinctive meanings – in which event misadventure might be thought the more appropriate of the two in the circumstances of the present case … (2) Any of the following expressions 'Abuse of volatile substances,' 'solvent abuse,' 'sniffing Tippex thinners,' 'inhalation of Tippex thinners.' (3) Any of the above terms could properly be used in combination. Thus it would be perfectly lawful to enter a verdict of 'accidental death resulting from the inhalation of Tippex thinners,' or 'solvent abuse: inhalation of Tippex thinners.'*

INDUSTRIAL DISEASE

In R (BP Chemicals) v HM Coroner for South Glamorgan (1987) 151 JP 799 the Court considered the case of a person who had worked approximately 250 to 300 yards from a processing plant that had manufactured vinyl chloride monomer. That substance was known to cause angiosarcoma of the liver in someone exposed to it.

The Court confirmed that the conclusion of 'industrial disease' was not limited to a list of specific diseases. At 803G:

> "*I am far from satisfied that a jury should be restrained from returning a verdict of industrial disease except in cases where those narrow criteria are satisfied … 'industrial disease' is just one of a list of suggested verdicts, and it would be somewhat surprising if it had a particular refined meaning. Of course I recognise that r.43 of the Coroners Rules does offer a definition of 'industrial disease' by reference to what is now the Social Security Act 1975 …*
>
> *[…]*
>
> *…on the facts of this case Mrs. Durbin never had [a disease listed in the Social Security Act 1975] but in my judgment once the jury was satisfied that she died from angiosarcoma of the liver contracted as a result of exposure to VCM whilst in the employ of B.P.Chemicals … then, unless there was no evidence to support that conclusion, it was open to the jury to return a verdict of industrial disease.*"

LAWFUL/UNLAWFUL KILLING

Lawful killing comprises those cases where a person is not killed illegally, such as a person who is shot lawfully by police officers in the execution of their duty. A recent example is the conclusion of 'lawful killing' at the inquest into the death of Usman Khan, the convicted terrorist who stabbed two people and injured others at an attack on the Fishmongers' Hall in November 2019. Mr Khan was shot by police officers on London Bridge, acting under instruction to deliver a 'critical shot' after legitimate fears that Mr Khan was carrying an explosive device which he was about to detonate.

Unlawful killing comprises those deaths which are caused by criminal offences of (1) murder; (2) manslaughter (including corporate manslaughter); and (3) infanticide[7].

The Chief Coroner has produced a Law Sheet which assists with this conclusion: Law Sheet No.1 *Unlawful Killing*. There is an important caveat to that, however; paragraphs 30 to 33 of that Law Sheet indicate that 'unlawful killing' must be proven to the criminal standard of proof. Certainly at the time of the last revision of the Law Sheet, that was correct: both 'unlawful killing' and 'suicide' needed to be proven to the criminal standard of proof.

However, that long-standing principle has been overturned by the relatively recent Supreme Court case of *R (on the application of Maughan) v HM Senior Coroner for Oxfordshire* (2020) UKSC 46, considered further below.

At paragraphs 35 to 42 of the Law Sheet, the Chief Coroner considers cases involving death caused by driving. In some cases a vehicle is used as a weapon of assault, and driven at a person with the intent to kill, cause really serious harm or to cause lesser harm. In those cases, the Law Sheet

---

[7] Chief Coroner's Law Sheet No.1 *Unlawful Killing*, revised 18 January 2016

indicates, a conclusion of unlawful killing at an inquest could be appropriate.

In other cases, however, such as the 'hit and run' type cases, it may be that a conclusion of 'accident' or 'misadventure' would be the correct conclusions – or, indeed, the comparatively new conclusion of 'road traffic collision'.

R (on the application of Maughan) v HM Senior Coroner for Oxfordshire (2020) UKSC 46

This case concerned an inquest into the death of a prisoner who had died by hanging in his prison cell. At the inquest, the principle issues were whether the man had intended to kill himself and whether the prison authorities had caused or contributed to his death.

The coroner decided that there was insufficient evidence to enable the jury to safely reach a short-form conclusion of suicide on the criminal standard of proof. As a result, the jury made a narrative statement of the circumstances of the deceased's death. This included their finding that, on the balance of probabilities, the deceased had intended to kill himself and increased vigilance by the authorities would not have prevented his suicide. The deceased's brother judicially reviewed this decision, arguing that the coroner erred in applying the criminal standard. The Divisional Court dismissed the application; the Court of Appeal upheld that dismissal. The matter then went to the Supreme Court.

The Supreme Court, however, delivered a significant decision that both 'suicide' and 'unlawful killing' were to be held to the civil standard of proof in inquest proceedings. Whilst no standard of proof had ever been enshrined in statute, the long-standing principle had been that those two conclusions were to be held to a higher standard of proof than all others. Indeed, the notes to the Record of Inquest Form referred to a criminal standard of proof for both those conclusions. This was, therefore, a fairly groundbreaking decision in the landscape of coronial law.

At paragraphs 93 to 97, having concluded that the standard of proof for a finding of 'suicide' should be the civil standard (for the reasoning, see the 'suicide' heading below):

> "*93. In my judgment, the short form conclusions of unlawful killing and suicide cannot satisfactorily be distinguished with respect to the standard of proof. As Davis LJ accepted, both such decisions contrast with the standard applying to narrative statements and different standards of proof may therefore confusingly apply to different conclusions within the same inquest. It is said that it would not promote public confidence in the legal system if a conclusion of unlawful killing is reached in an inquest on the civil standard, and a prosecution is mounted as a result which then fails. But that can happen in any event, even if the existing criminal standard is maintained, and it is at least as likely that public confidence in the legal system will be diminished if the evidence at the inquest cannot lead to clear findings on a balance of probabilities. It would appear to the public as if the system has conspired to prevent the truth from being available to them. It seems to me that the public are likely to understand that there is difference between a finding at an inquest and one at a criminal trial where the accused has well-established rights to participate actively in the process.*
>
> *94. Moreover, if there appears to be a risk that criminal proceedings will be brought before an inquest has been completed, the inquest can be adjourned, and in some circumstances must be adjourned (see the 2009 Act, Schedule 1). In that way the person who is at risk of prosecution is protected against a short form conclusion reached on a civil standard which is unfavourable to him.*
>
> *95. The person implicated in the conclusion of unlawful killing is equally liable to suffer prejudice from the findings by way of narrative statement, which can be found on a balance of probabilities. They may equally point a finger at him. In addition, as Mr Straw points out, the accused would be in the same position in an inquest as he already is if civil proceedings are brought against him.*

96. In summary, a common standard applying to both unlawful killing and suicide is more consistent with principle and removes an inherent inconsistency in the determinations made at an inquest. It reflects the general rule for the standard of proof in civil proceedings. In short, it seems to me that the arguments in favour of applying the rule that in most civil proceedings the civil standard will apply are stronger than those against, and that this Court should take the opportunity of so deciding.

Conclusion

97. I would dismiss this appeal. The standard of proof for all short form conclusions at an inquest is the balance of probabilities."

<u>*R (Wilkinson) v HM Coroner for Greater Manchester South District* (2012) EWHC 2755</u>

In this case, the Court considered whether evidence of causing death by careless driving was capable of justifying a verdict of 'unlawful killing' at an inquest. We know that Chief Coroner's Law Sheet No.1 now makes clear that death by driving cases are not intended to fall under the ambit of 'unlawful killing' apart from where the car has been used as a weapon in commission of murder or manslaughter.

This case sets out the reasoning behind that principle. At paragraphs 63 to 64:

"63. In our judgement, the main purpose of having a verdict of unlawful killing is to distinguish between those cases where there has been an accident of some kind (where, of course, someone may be to blame for it, even with some degree of criminality) and those cases where it would be an abuse of language to describe the events leading to death as simply an accident. Someone killed by murder, manslaughter or infanticide is killed either intentionally or by some obviously criminal state of mind on the part of, or some negligence of the grossest kind by, the author of the killing. Someone killed by careless driving is killed as a result of an accident arising from, or at least

contributed to by, the actions of the careless driver. Those actions may give rise to criminal consequences, but given the essential purpose and scope of an inquest, it is neither necessary nor appropriate to investigate and record that conclusion.

64. Applying those basic tenets of coroner law leads to the principled conclusion that causing death by careless or inconsiderate driving should not be treated as "unlawful killing" for the purposes of the conclusion of an inquest whatever conclusion may be reached in other contexts."

NATURAL CAUSES

Death by natural causes will tend to encompass deaths caused by ailments or natural disease. Of course, by virtue of the fact that the coroner has decided to conduct an inquest, the death may have initially been thought to have been unnatural, violent or at least unknown (see Chapter 3). As the evidence has emerged during the inquest, however, a clearer picture almost inevitably gathers. Much of the case law relating to the meaning of the word 'natural' has arisen from the coroner's refusal to hold an inquest, on the grounds that they believe the death to have been the result of natural causes. If this is a possible conclusion in your case, then, it may be helpful to return to the analysis of the key cases around the meaning of the word 'natural' in Chapter 3.

OPEN CONCLUSION

In brief, an open conclusion is reached when there is insufficient evidence to record any other conclusion. It is established principle, though, that an open conclusion is to be a last resort.

In Re Tabarn (1998) EWHC (Admin) 8

The applicant challenged the coroner's conclusion of 'death by natural causes' at the inquest into the death of her daughter. The deceased had died following participation in a hypnotism stage act. The cause of death was pulmonary oedema and there were indications that the deceased had suffered a fit. The applicant had gathered evidence from a highly qualified specialist in the field of hypnosis and its risk to health to contend that the coroner should have recorded an open verdict and requested a new inquest.

In dismissing the application the Court found that a properly directed jury would have been bound to produce the same verdict. A Home Office enquiry had fully investigated stage hypnosis and no useful purpose would be served by a fresh inquest. In setting out its decision, the Court had the following to say about open verdicts at 46 to 47 (*per* Brown LJ):

> "*46. The important point to make is that open verdicts are to be discouraged, save where strictly necessary. As is said in para 13(32) of Jervis on Coroners 11th Ed p253:*
>
> > *'If there is insufficient evidence to record any of the other suggested conclusions, an 'open verdict' may be recorded. This includes the case where there is evidence that it fails to reach the required standard of proof. It should be noted that an open verdict is thus only to be used in the last resort if there is insufficient evidence to enable the coroner or the jury to reach one of the other conclusions. The fact that there may be uncertainty as to other parts of the inquisition, for example as to the precise cause, time or place of death, does not authorise recording an open verdict if there is sufficient evidence to record how the deceased came by his death. In other words the coroner or jury should not fail to reach a positive conclusion merely because there was some doubt on some minor point.'*
>
> *47. I do not suggest that the issue as to the relevance of hypnosis here can be discarded as 'some minor point', and what is to be emphasises the point that an open verdict should only be used as a last resort, notably when the coroner is simply unable to reach any conclusion on the balance of probabilities as between two competing verdicts.*"

ROAD TRAFFIC COLLISION

This is a comparatively new conclusion; it was included for the first time in the 2013 Inquests Rules.

The Chief Coroner's Law Sheet No.1 *Unlawful Killing* touches upon some useful guidance in relation to the conclusion of 'road traffic collision'. At paragraphs 40 to 41 of Law Sheet No.1, having earlier indicated that where a car being used as a weapon amounting to murder or manslaughter would likely lead to a conclusion of 'unlawful killing':

> "*40. If the road death case did not, under the old law, involve manslaughter, the normal verdict in an inquest, should have been accident (see Wilkinson above). Misadventure might at times have felt more appropriate. However, Schedule 2 of the Coroners (Inquests) Rules 2013 includes for the first time a short-form conclusion of road traffic collision, which for most families may sound better than accident. In addition to the findings of act in Box 3 of the Record of Inquest and the recording of a short-form conclusion in Box 4, or as an alternative to a short-form conclusion, a brief narrative conclusion may be entered in Box 4, if appropriate.*
>
> *41. Where a short-form conclusion is used in some cases of bad driving falling short of manslaughter, coroners may feel that some words should be used in addition to accident or road traffic collision in order to alleviate any bereaved family's feeling that the outcome is disproportionate to the incident. Coroners will choose their own words. The use of clear, brief, neutral, findings of fact (in Box 3) may be helpful. For example, 'The unknown driver left the scene without stopping. He had been travelling at high speed down an ill-lit narrow street, knocking into parked cards, before he struck and knocked down the deceased who was walking along the side of the road, causing the injuries from which he died. Those are my findings of fact. I shall therefore record the formal conclusion [under the law / as required by law] as accident or road traffic collision. (Box 4)*".

STILLBIRTH

This conclusion was introduced in this form by the 2013 Inquests Rules; previously this conclusion was called 'want of attention at birth'.

The current Chief Coroner (as of 5 October 2023) HHJ Tomas Teague KC has produced Guidance No.45 *Stillbirth, and Live Birth Following Termination of Pregnancy*, dated 2 February 2023.

This provides guidance as to the coroner's jurisdiction, notification of death, how to establish whether there has been a live birth, live births after termination and notification requirements.

In relation to jurisdiction, at Guidance No.45 paragraphs 3 to 6:

> "*3. For the purposes of death registration, a stillborn child is one which has issued forth from its mother after the 24th week of pregnancy and which did not at any time after being completely expelled from its mother breathe or show any other signs of life.*
>
> *4. Coroners do not have jurisdiction to conduct an investigation concerning a foetus or a stillborn child, as where there has not been an independent life, there has not legally been a death.*
>
> *5. However, a child who is born showing signs of life, whether that is prior to the 24th week of pregnancy or after it, has had an independent life and that child's death must be investigated if section 1 Coroners and Justice Act 2009 is engaged. This is so even where the mother's pregnancy was intentionally terminated.*
>
> *6. Where there is doubt over whether a child was born alive, that is a matter for the coroner to determine*".

Paragraph 12 of Guidance No.45 tells us that to be considered to have been born alive, a child must:

- Have issued completely from its mother's body. It does not matter whether the birth was vaginal or by caesarean section, and the placenta need not have been delivered, nor umbilical cord have been cut;

- Have shown signs of life. There is no formal definition as to what constitutes a sign of life, and coroners may need to obtain a medical opinion. Signs can include: breathing, crying, sustained gasps, a heartbeat, a pulsing umbilical cord and making definite movement of voluntary muscles.

By virtue of paragraph 14 of Guidance No.45, where there is doubt about whether a child was born alive or was stillborn, a coroner can either make preliminary inquiries to try to establish the position, or can begin an investigation. A coroner does not have to be satisfied on the balance of probabilities that the child was born alive before an investigation can be commenced.

A recent example of such an investigation being commenced, and in fact proceeding through to inquest, without proof positive that the baby was born alive is the inquest into the death of Aisha Cleary. That inquest concluded in July 2023, having lasted a month. Aisha Cleary's mother was a vulnerable 18-year old prison inmate. She went into labour one evening and used the intercom in her cell to urgently request a nurse or ambulance. The officer who answered that call did not in fact summon a nurse or ambulance. Indeed, nobody attended the mother that night. The following morning, the mother was found to have given birth alone during the night. The baby was dead. The coroner concluded that the evidence was insufficient to determine whether or not the baby had been stillborn or born alive and subsequently died. Notwithstanding his inability to make that determination, he had found that Article 2 of the ECHR was engaged where it was possible that Aisha Cleary had been born alive and where there was evidence that serious systemic failures had contributed to her death.

Whilst this case has not made its way to the higher courts, it may pave the way for coroners in future such inquests to consider that they can fully investigate the death even without knowing whether the child was born alive or was in fact stillborn (with the latter ordinarily meaning they have no jurisdiction).

SUICIDE

The conclusion of 'suicide' was, until the 2020 Supreme Court case of *Maughan*, *supra*, subject to the criminal standard of proof – i.e. the coroner / jury had to be 'sure' that death was by suicide.

The 'unlawful killing' heading above covered the facts of *Maughan* in some detail, so it is worth referring to that section should you be considering a conclusion of 'suicide' in a particular inquest. To avoid repetition, set out below is simply the particular reasoning of the Supreme Court in relation to the standard of proof for a conclusion of 'suicide'.

R (on the application of Maughan) v HM Senior Coroner for Oxfordshire (2020) UKSC 46

At paragraphs 68 to 77, having set out at paragraphs 60 to 61 the numerous cases in which the Divisional Court or Court of Appeal held that the criminal standard applied to conclusions of suicide:

> "*68. I fully accept that it may be an anxious cause of concern to the family of the deceased if the evidential standard for the short form conclusion of suicide is not the criminal standard but the lower civil standard. However, the issue of the correct standard of proof for a short form conclusion of suicide has to be decided on the basis of legal principle. The position is that to hold that a criminal standard applies is out of line not only with narrative conclusions but also with the principle applying to civil proceedings generally. I see no reason why the normal legal principles should not apply. On the contrary there are good reasons why they should apply. Short form conclusions on the basis of the civil standard may for instance enhance the recording of suicides*

and assist research for the future. In my judgment the arguments for doing so are compelling. I explain my reasons for so concluding below.

(1) On legal principle, the civil standard should apply, and the common law does not demonstrate any cogent reason for not applying that principle

69. The principle is clear and it is that in civil proceedings the civil standard of proof should apply. There may be cases where it does not so apply, for example, contempt and forfeiture, but they are rare. These particular situations involve risk to liberty and loss of property, both keenly protected by the common law.

70. None of the many cases on dealing with the standard of proof for suicide cited here or below is binding on us. I have considered them for the assistance which they can give to this court today in deciding what standard of proof the law requires. The assistance is somewhat limited. In, for example, R v West London Coroner, Ex p Gray, [1988] QB 467, the Divisional Court was not bound by any earlier decision for the reasons which the Divisional Court in this case gave (para 59). So the Divisional Court in Gray had to articulate their own reasoning but they did not do so, perhaps because they had been misled into thinking that the earlier case of R v City of London Coroner, Ex p Barber [1975] 1 WLR 310 was decisive of the issue. The Divisional Court simply came to the view that it was "unthinkable" that any lesser standard should apply (see para 60 of the Divisional Court's judgment in this case). It is as if the common law had accepted that the criminal standard applied because of the links between coronial proceedings and criminal proceedings, the serious consequences of suicide (which at one time led to the denial of normal burial rites and the barbaric practice of burial on the highway impaled by a stake), and the then generally prevailing societal norms attaching stigma to suicide. There are rare occasions when the reason for a rule has disappeared but the rule remains. This would appear to be one of those situations.

71. The rule cannot be left as it is. As the Divisional Court first pointed out, if the appellant is right and the criminal standard is applied to the findings which pertain to the elements of suicide, then some conclusions will be reached on one basis and some on another within a single inquest. A system of fact-finding on this basis is internally inconsistent and unprincipled and does not meet the standards of a modern, principled legal system. It is quite different from the situation which Woolf LJ (as he then was) (with whom Lord Donaldson MR and Stocker LJ agreed) considered and found satisfactory in McCurbin. In that case, Woolf LJ saw no difficulty in the jury considering unlawful killing on the basis of the criminal standard and if not sure, misadventure on the civil standard:

> *"I am quite satisfied that, in a case where it is open to a jury, as a result of a coroner's inquest, to come to a verdict of unlawful killing, the appropriate direction which the coroner should give to the jury is the simple one that they should be satisfied beyond all reasonable doubt or, as sometimes said, satisfied so that they are sure. That provides clear guidance to the coroner's jury which they will be able to follow, and it is not necessary for them to be involved with sliding scales which are more appropriate for a judge than a jury.*

It is true that, in many cases where it is open to a coroner's jury to find a verdict of unlawful killing, they may also have to consider the question of death by misadventure. However, in my view, this does not and should not give rise to problems. The coroner should indicate to the jury that they should approach, initially, the question as to whether or not they are satisfied so that they are sure that this is unlawful killing. If they come to the conclusion that it is unlawful killing, there is no need for them to go on to consider death by misadventure. But, if they come to the conclusion that it is not unlawful killing, they are not satisfied so that they are sure that that verdict is appropriate, then they will consider the question of misadventure and, in so doing, they do not need to bear in mind the heavy standard of proof which is required for unlawful killing. They can approach the matter on the basis of the balance of probabilities. The situation is that, just as it is important that a jury should not bring in a verdict of suicide unless they are sure, likewise they should not bring in a verdict of unlawful killing unless they are sure." (p 728)

72. Finally, on this point, the civil standard still results in safeguarding the interests of those adversely affected by the conclusion. As the Divisional Court pointed out (para 56), a conclusion on the balance of probabilities still involves showing that it is more likely than not that the deceased took his own life and intended so to do. It is not enough for the coroner or the jury to think that because certain possibilities (for example, unlawful killing by a person unknown) can be discounted, that suicide must have occurred.

(2) The criminal standard may lead to suicides being under-recorded and to lessons not being learnt.

73. The retention of the criminal standard for the short form conclusion of suicide is likely to lead to the assessment of when, where and in what circumstances did the deceased meet his death being left in a partially complete and incoherent way, which may give an inaccurate understanding of the position.

74. The reasons for suicide are often complex. It is important not to adopt a stereotypical attitude here as elsewhere. Society needs to understand the causes and to try and prevent suicides occurring. Statistics are the means whereby this can be done. If a criminal burden of proof is required, suicide is likely to be under-recorded. This is especially worrying in the case of state-related deaths. If there is an open verdict because the criminal standard of proof cannot be achieved, the circumstances of the case have to be analysed before it can be included in any statistics to show the true number of suicides. There is a considerable public interest in accurate suicide statistics as they may reveal a need for social and medical care in areas not previously regarded as significant. Each suicide determination can help others by revealing how suicide risks may be managed in future. I accept that to some extent policy makers and researchers can seek to mitigate the under-recording of cases by examining cases of open conclusions but they may not be able to do so accurately and lowering the standard of proof would be a more satisfactory way of getting accurate figures.

(3) The changing role of inquests and changing societal attitudes and expectations confirm the need to review the standard of proof.

75. I have answered the question on this appeal in terms of legal principle but it may be asked why the standard of proof should now be challenged and why it is thought that a different and lower standard should now apply. In answer I should like to record some significant changes in the legislative background and in societal attitudes and expectations that have occurred in recent years.

76. As to legislative background, suicide used to be a crime, but it ceased to be such in 1961. Section 1 of the Suicide Act 1961 enacts that: "The rule of law whereby it is a crime for a person to commit suicide is hereby abrogated." Although the offence has been abolished, it is still a crime to encourage or assist a person to commit suicide (Suicide Act 1961, section 2).

77. There has been an unmistakeable change in society's understanding and attitude to suicide. This change is charted by Lloyd LJ in Kirkham v Chief Constable of the Greater Manchester Police [1990] 2 QB 283. In that case, the court was faced with the argument that there was a defence to a claim for damages against a prison authority where a person had committed suicide in circumstances where it was alleged that the prison authorities had been negligent, on the basis of the defence of ex turpi causa, namely that it was contrary to public policy for a person who had committed suicide to recover damages. Lloyd LJ rejected that defence, holding:

> *"It is apparent from these authorities that the ex turpi causa defence is not confined to criminal conduct. So we cannot adopt the simple approach favoured by the judge. We have to ask*

ourselves the much more difficult question whether to afford relief in such a case as this, arising, as it does, directly out of a man's suicide, would affront the public conscience, or, as I would prefer to say, shock the ordinary citizen. I have come to the conclusion that the answer should be in the negative. I would give two reasons. In the first place the Suicide Act 1961 does more than abolish the crime of suicide. It is symptomatic of a change in the public attitude to suicide generally. It is no longer regarded with the same abhorrence as it once was. It is, or course, impossible for us to say how far the change in the public attitude has gone. But that there has been a change is beyond doubt. The fact that aiding and abetting suicide remains a crime under section 2 of the Suicide Act 1961 does not diminish the force of the argument. The second reason is that in at least two decided cases courts have awarded damages following a suicide or attempted suicide. In Selfe v Ilford and District Hospital Management Committee, The Times, 26 November 1970, Hinchcliffe J awarded the plaintiff damages against a hospital for failing to take proper precautions when they knew that the plaintiff was a suicide risk. In Pigney v Pointer's Transport Services Ltd [1957] 1 WLR 1121, to which I have already referred, Pilcher J. awarded damages to the dependants of a suicide under the Fatal Accidents Act 1846. Moreover, in Hyde v Tameside Area Health Authority, Court of Appeal (Civil Division) Transcript No 130 of 1981 another hospital case, the judge awarded £200,000 damages in respect of an unsuccessful suicide attempt. The Court of Appeal allowed the defendant's appeal, on the ground that there had been no negligence on the part of the hospital, but not on the ground that the plaintiff's cause of action arose ex turpi causa. Selfe and Pigney are not binding on us. But they are important for this reason. They show, or appear to show, that the public conscience was not affronted. It did not occur to anyone to argue in either case that the granting of a remedy would shock the ordinary citizen; nor did it occur to the court.

> *For the above reason I would hold that the defence of ex turpi causa is not available in these cases, at any rate where, as here, there is medical evidence that the suicide is not in full possession of his mind. To entertain the plaintiff's claim in such a case as the present would not, in my view, affront the public conscience, or shock the ordinary citizen." (p 291)"*

And at paragraph 81:

> "*81. The role of inquests has also changed (see paras 8 to 10 above). Inquests are concerned today not with criminal justice but with the investigation of deaths. They take a new and different purpose in a case such as this.*"

Re Steponaviciene's Application for Judicial Review (2020) NICA 61

The appellant was the mother of the deceased. She had applied to judicially review the ruling of a coroner that the jury should apply the civil standard of proof when considering whether her son had died by suicide. That application was dismissed, and she accordingly appealed against the dismissal.

In dismissing the appeal, the Court of Appeal followed the Supreme Court's decision in *Maughan, supra*, holding at paragraph 8:

> "*8. Suicide requires proof and should not be presumed. That principle was supported by all of the Justices. There is, however, no basis upon which this court could distinguish this case or fail to follow this binding authority from the Supreme Court despite the persuasive judgment in dissent by Lord Kerr with whom Lord Reed agreed. Accordingly, it must follow that the appeal should be dismissed.*"

A 'BOLT-ON': NEGLECT

Neglect is not a finding which may stand on its own as a conclusion[8]; accordingly it is not listed in the list of short-form conclusions in the Record of Inquest. It is, though, a finding which may be recorded as part of the inquest conclusion.

In *Jamieson* (see Chapter 6 on scope of inquests for detailed discussion of this case), neglect was defined at 25(9):

> "*(9) Neglect in this context means a gross failure to provide adequate nourishment or liquid, or provide or procure basic medical attention or shelter or warmth for someone in a dependent position (because of youth, age, illness or incarceration) who cannot provide it for himself. Failure to provide medical attention for a dependent person whose physical condition is such as to show that he obviously needs it may amount to neglect. So it may be if it is the dependent person's mental condition which obviously calls for medical attention (as it would, for example, if a mental nurse observed that a patient had a propensity to swallow razor blades and failed to report this propensity to a doctor, in a case where the patient had no intention to cause himself injury but did thereafter swallow razor blades with fatal results). In both cases the crucial consideration will be what the dependent person's condition, whether physical or mental, appeared to be.*"

At 26(12):

> "*(12) Neither neglect nor self-neglect should ever form any part of any verdict unless a clear and direct causal connection is established between the conduct so described and the cause of death.*"

Some key points taken from the caselaw in relation to 'neglect' are:

---

[8] see *Jamieson*, discussed in Chapter 6, at 25(10)

- A 'gross failure' is not limited to incidents where the carer has failed to take any action[9];

- The medical staff's view was relevant to the question of 'neglect' but does not rule out 'neglect'[10];

- Omissions on the part of medical practitioners are capable of forming part of the picture of neglect[11];

- A failure to procure effective medical treatment could be a gross failure for the purposes of neglect[12];

- A failure to follow proper and routine procedures might amount to neglect[13];

- The question is whether the carer should have realised the need for action in all the circumstances[14];

- This does not mean that every incorrect clinical judgment amounts to neglect. If doctors consider all the issues and ask themselves the right question(s), an erroneous decision may not amount to neglect[15];

---

9 (*R (Davies) v HM Deputy Coroner for Birmingham* (2003) EWHC 618 Admin)

10 *(R (Scott) v HM Coroner for Inner West London* (2001) EWHC Admin 105);

11 Scott, *supra*

12 *R v HM Coroner for Wiltshire ex p Clegg* (1996) 161 JP 521)

13 *R v Inner North London Coroner ex p Touche* (2001) EWCA Civ 383; *R v HM Coroner for Swansea and Gower ex p Tristram* (2000) 164 JP 191

14 *Tristram, supra*

15 *R (Mumford) v HM Coroner for Reading* (2002) EWHC Admin 2184)

- There is no precise dividing line between a gross failure to provide basic medical attention and a failure to provide medical attention. It is fact dependent[16];

- It is not the role of the inquest to criticise every twist and turn of a patient's medical treatment[17];

- Rare circumstances can exist where it is appropriate to make a finding that neglect was a cause that contributed to the death of a person who killed himself or herself[18].

16 *R (Nicholls) v HM Coroner for City of Liverpool* (2001) EWHC Admin 992

17 *Nicholls, supra*

18 *R (Clegg) v HM Coroner for Wiltshire* (1997) 161 JP 521

PART FOUR

AFTER THE INQUEST

CHAPTER FOURTEEN

PREVENTION OF FUTURE DEATHS REPORTS

WHAT IS A PREVENTION OF FUTURE DEATHS REPORT?

A 'Prevention of Future Deaths report' is, as its name indicates, a report created by the coroner which is designed to encourage changes in order to prevent further deaths occurring.

Chief Coroner's Guidance No.5 *Reports to Prevent Future Deaths* (revised, as of 20 November 2020) emphasises the importance of Prevention of Future Death Reports (or "PFDs") at paragraph 2:

> "*2. PFDs are vitally important if society is to learn from deaths. Coroners have a duty to decide how somebody came by their death. They also have a statutory duty (rather than simply a power), where appropriate, to report about deaths with a view to preventing future deaths. And a bereaved family wants to be able to say: 'His death was tragic and terrible, but at least it's less likely to happen to somebody else.' PFDs are not intended as a punishment; they are made for the benefit of the public.*"

As to the purpose of the reports, Guidance No.5 at paragraph 4 states:

> "*Broadly speaking, PFDs should be intended to improve public health, welfare and safety.*"

A Prevention of Future Deaths report may also complete the state's duty to inquire fully in an Article 2 inquest. It does not follow, though, that a report is mandatory simply because an inquest is an Article 2 inquest[19].

WHEN DOES A CORONER MAKE A REPORT?

By virtue of paragraph 7 of Schedule 5 to the 2009 Act, the coroner is under a duty to make a report in the following circumstances:

"*7*

(1) Where—

(a) a senior coroner has been conducting an investigation under this Part into a person's death,

(b) anything revealed by the investigation gives rise to a concern that circumstances creating a risk of other deaths will occur, or will continue to exist, in the future, and

(c) in the coroner's opinion, action should be taken to prevent the occurrence or continuation of such circumstances, or to eliminate or reduce the risk of death created by such circumstances,

the coroner must report the matter to a person who the coroner believes may have power to take such action.

(2) A person to whom a senior coroner makes a report under this paragraph must give the senior coroner a written response to it.

(3) A copy of a report under this paragraph, and of the response to it, must be sent to the Chief Coroner."

---

[19] Paragraph 6 of Guidance No.5

Regulation 28 of the 2013 Investigations Regulations sets out the procedure once a coroner comes under a duty to make a report (*note:* it is by virtue of this Regulation that Prevention of Future Death reports are sometimes referred to as 'Regulation 28 Reports'):

> "***28.— Report on action to prevent other deaths***
>
> *(1) This regulation applies where a coroner is under a duty under paragraph 7(1) of Schedule 5 to make a report to prevent other deaths.*
>
> *(2) In this regulation, a reference to "a report" means a report to prevent other deaths made by the coroner.*
>
> *(3) A report may not be made until the coroner has considered all the documents, evidence and information that in the opinion of the coroner are relevant to the investigation.*
>
> *(4) The coroner—*
>
> > *(a) must send a copy of the report to the Chief Coroner and every interested person who in the coroner's opinion should receive it;*
> >
> > *(b) must send a copy of the report to the appropriate Local Safeguarding Children Board or as the case may be the appropriate Safeguarding Children Board (which have the same meaning as in regulation 24(3)) where the coroner believes the deceased was under the age of 18; and*
> >
> > *(c) may send a copy of the report to any other person who the coroner believes may find it useful or of interest.*
>
> *(5) On receipt of a report the Chief Coroner may—*
>
> > *(a) publish a copy of the report, or a summary of it, in such manner as the Chief Coroner thinks fit; and*
> >
> > *(b) send a copy of the report to any person who the Chief Coroner believes may find it useful or of interest.*"

At paragraphs 7 and 8 of Guidance No.5 the Chief Coroner provides the following assistance in determining whether a coroner is under a duty to make a report:

> "*7. In considering whether they are under a duty to make a PFD report, coroners should focus on the current position. This will normally be the position at the end of the inquest unless, unusually, consideration is being given to making a PFD report before the resumed inquest. Coroners should consider evidence and information about relevant changes made since the death or plans to implement such changes. If a potential PFD recipient has already implemented appropriate action to address the risk of future fatalities, the coroner may not need to need to make a report to that body. Whether a coroner needs to do so or not is a judicial decision for the coroner to make on a case by case basis taking into consideration all the circumstances. However, a report to a relevant national organisation to highlight the issues more widely may still be appropriate provided the evidence suggests that the risk of future fatalities may arise nationally and the coroner believes that national action should be taken. In other cases, action may not yet have been fully implemented by the potential PFD recipient, but such action may be ongoing, or the coroner may be told that a decision has been taken to take specific action in the near future. Occasionally, the need to take action may only have arisen from the evidence emerging at the inquest itself. Whether a PFD report is required in these cases will be highly fact sensitive, depending upon the circumstances of each individual case. Relevant factors may include the nature of the commitment to take action, any evidence in support of it, and the coroner's assessment of the organisation's understanding of, and commitment to addressing, the area of concern.*
>
> *8. It is for the coroner to decide whether the duty arises in any particular instance, having considered the matter as a whole and heard representations if there are any. The coroner may be assisted by considering the potential recipient in the context of any other PFDs sent to that individual or organisation. The coroner is a local judge and is able to consider local trends.*"

The Prevention of Future Deaths report will normally be made after the inquest is concluded[20]. However where the coroner concludes that there is an urgent need for action she or he may report with a view to action being taken without delay. Given that the concern may arise from 'anything revealed by the investigation' – rather than 'anything revealed by the inquest' – that leaves room for a report to be made during the investigation but before the inquest[21].

CONTENT OF THE PREVENTION OF FUTURE DEATHS REPORT

There is a template for the report, a copy of which is annexed to Guidance No.5. In brief, the coroner must set out the details of the investigation (and inquest) and the circumstances of the death. The coroner then lists their concerns in box 5.

In relation to those concerns, Guidance No.5 emphasises at paragraph 26 that:

> *"26. This part is the essence of a report to prevent future deaths. The coroner should express clearly, simply and 'in neutral and non-contentious terms' the factual basis for each concern (R v Shrewsbury Coroner's Court, ex parte British Parachute Association (1988) 152 JP 123)."*

Coroners should be careful to base their report on clear evidence at the inquest, or on clear information during the investigation. They should express clearly and simply what that information or evidence is and ensure that a bereaved family's expectations are not unrealistically raised[22].

---

[20] Chief Coroners Guidance No.5 at paragraph 13

[21] Chief Coroners Guidance No.5 at paragraph 14

[22] Chief Coroners Guidance No.5 at paragraph 28

Prevention of Future Deaths reports should not apportion blame, be defamatory, prejudice law enforcement action or the administration of justice, affect national security, put anyone's safety at risk or breach data protection (such as by naming children or breaching medical confidentiality)[23]. Coroners should also not make any other observations of any kind, however well intentioned, outside the scope of the report[24]. Coroners should also, at all times, use moderate, neutral, well-tempered language, befitting a judge. This applies to public hearings as well as correspondence and reports[25].

Having expressed their concerns, the report should state (in box 6 of the template) that in the coroner's opinion action should be taken, and that the coroner believes that person/organisation has the power to take such action. The coroner should not, though, recommend what that action should be but can highlight the area of concern and draw attention to it[26].

Note that once a report has been sent, the coroner has no power to withdraw it. The appropriate remedy for correcting any mistake of fact in the report is by responding to it[27].

RESPONSES TO THE REPORT

Regulation 29 of the 2013 Investigations Rules sets out provisions relating to responses to the report:

> "***29.— Response to a report on action to prevent other deaths***

---

23 Chief Coroners Guidance No.5 at paragraph 29

24 Chief Coroners Guidance No.5 at paragraph 30

25 Chief Coroners Guidance No.5 at paragraph 31

26 Chief Coroners Guidance No.5 at paragraph 32

27 Chief Coroners Guidance No.5 at paragraph 39, paragraph 7(1) of Schedule 5 to the 2009 Act and *R(Siddiqui & Paeprer-Rohricht) v HM Assistant Coroner for East London* (28 September 2017) Admin Court CO/2892/2017

(1) This regulation applies where a person is under a duty to give a response to a report to prevent other deaths made in accordance with paragraph 7(1) of Schedule 5.

(2) In this regulation, a reference to "a report" means a report to prevent other deaths made by the coroner.

(3) The response to a report must contain—

> *(a) details of any action that has been taken or which it is proposed will be taken by the person giving the response or any other person whether in response to the report or otherwise and set out a timetable of the action taken or proposed to be taken; or*
>
> *(b) an explanation as to why no action is proposed.*

(4) The response must be provided to the coroner who made the report within 56 days of the date on which the report is sent.

(5) The coroner who made the report may extend the period referred to in paragraph (4) (even if an application for extension is made after the time for compliance has expired).

(6) On receipt of a response to a report the coroner—

> *(a) must send a copy of the response to the report to the Chief Coroner;*
>
> *(b) must send a copy to any interested persons who in the coroner's opinion should receive it; and*
>
> *(c) may send a copy of the response to any other person who the coroner believes may find it useful or of interest.*

(7) On receipt of a copy under paragraph (6)(a) the Chief Coroner may—

> *(a) publish a copy of the response, or a summary of it, in such manner as the Chief Coroner thinks fit; and*
>
> *(b) send a copy of the response to any person who the Chief Coroner believes may find it useful or of interest (other than a person who has been sent a copy of the response under paragraph (6)(b) or (c)).*
>
> *(8) A person giving a response to a report may make written representations to the coroner about—*
>
> *(a) the release of the response; or*
>
> *(b) the publication of the response.*
>
> *(9) Representations under paragraph (8) must be made to the coroner no later than the time when the response to the report to prevent other deaths is provided to the coroner under paragraph (4).*
>
> *(10) The coroner must pass any representations made under paragraph (8) to the Chief Coroner who may then consider those representations and decide whether there should be any restrictions on the release or publication of the response."*

Those who are required to provide a response, therefore, need not take action; if no action is taken, though, they must explain the reason(s) why.

TIME LIMITS

The time limits for issuing and responding to a report are as follows:

- The report should be sent out either: a) within 10 working days of the end of the inquest; or b) within 10 working days of the time before inquest, when the matter of concern is revealed and considered during the course of the investigation[28];

- A copy of the report must be sent to the Chief Coroner and to all interested persons who in the coroner's opinion should receive it[29];

- The person or organisation required to respond must do wo within 56 days, or longer if the coroner grants an extension[30].

RELEVANT CASES

Coroners Inquests into the London Bombings of 7 July 2005, *ruling of 6 May 2011*

This was the inquest into the deaths of 52 people on London public transport, after four suicide bombers detonated explosive devices in the Summer of 2005. The inquest was held before Hallet LJ. In her ruling of 6 May 2011, she considered the role of Prevention of Future Death reports at 15:

> *"First, the condition for the exercise of the power is that the coroner has a concern as to circumstances creating a risk to life. This is a relatively low threshold. The rule does not require, for example, that I have concluded or am satisfied that such circumstances exist. Second, the substance of the concern must be circumstances creating a risk to life, but those circumstances need not already exist at the time of the decision to make a report. The concern must be of a risk to life caused by present or future circumstances. Third, the concern must be based on evidence. Fourth, the coroner must be of the opinion that action should be taken to respond to the concern as to risk to life."*

[28] Chief Coroner's Guidance No.5 at paragraph 38

[29] Regulation 28(4)(a) of the 2013 Investigation Regulations

[30] Regulation 29$) and (5) of the 2013 Investigation Regulations

R (on the application of Gorani) v HM Assistant Coroner for Inner West London [2022] EWHC 1680 (Admin)

The applicants brought challenges to the coroner's decisions on various grounds, one of which was that the coroner erred in deciding not to make a Prevention of Future Death report without first hearing submissions from the interested persons.

In refusing the application, the Court stated at paragraphs 95 to 97:

> "*95. Schedule 5 imposes a duty to issue a report when the criteria set out in the schedule are met. In this regard, the 2009 Act changed the previous procedure; under the 1984 Rules, there was a power, but not a duty, to do so. But there is nothing in the wording of Schedule 5 which imposes a requirement on the Coroner to hear submission from interested persons before deciding whether or not the duty to report arises.*
>
> *96. Further, I can see no grounds to imply such an obligation, or for rejecting the Guidance of the Chief Coroner on the topic. An inquest remains an inquisitorial process and the duty here is one imposed on the coroner. It is in circumstances where she forms the opinion, in the light of the facts revealed by the investigation, that action is required that she is required to make a report. No doubt it will often be the case that a coroner will find it helpful to invite such submissions, but there is no obligation on her to do so.*
>
> *97. Given her findings and conclusions, her decision not to do so here was entirely reasonable.*"

R (on the application of Dillon) v HM Assistant Coroner for Rutland and North Leicestershire (2022) EWHC 318

The claimant applied for judicial review of the defendant coroner's refusal to make a report for the prevention of future deaths (PFD report) under the Coroners and Justice Act 2009 Sch.5 para.7.

The claimant was the prisoner's brother. In March 2018, shortly after the prison's healthcare department had closed for the day, the prisoner experienced breathing difficulties and called for assistance. The prison was in "patrol state", meaning all prisoners were locked in their cells with one prison officer on duty in each of the prison's six wings. The wing's officer attended but did not enter the cell because he believed three officers needed to be present to do so, unaware that he had a discretion to enter if there was an immediate risk to life. The officer radioed his manager for assistance; the manager attended eight minutes later with another officer and commenced cardiopulmonary resuscitation (CPR) as he was first aid trained. A "Code Blue" medical emergency was made to all officers, triggering the calling of an ambulance, which arrived 20 minutes later. The prisoner was pronounced dead shortly afterwards. An inquest jury found that the medical cause of death was unascertained and that any delay by prison officers in the commencement of CPR had not affected the prisoner's outcome.

At the time of the prisoner's death, there was no system of spot checks on officers undertaking patrol state duty to check their understanding of emergency procedures but spot checks were carried out during night duty. The coroner considered that spot checks could easily be expanded from night to patrol state and that she would only write a PFD report if such checks were not introduced. She noted that she did not have the power to enforce 24-hour healthcare or first aid training for all officers, but they were "ideal world scenarios" and she did not consider that the PFD threshold had been met. Her decision was challenged by way of judicial review.

The application was refused. In reaching their decision, the Court stated at paragraphs 71 to 72:

> *"71. We are not persuaded that the Coroner's reluctance to engage with what she regarded as "ideal world scenarios" was wrong or that resourcing issues were irrelevant in any event. The Coroner must by statute form an opinion as to whether "action should be taken" to prevent future deaths. In our judgment, these statutory words are*

sufficiently broad to entitle a coroner to consider what can practically be achieved – otherwise there is no real or actual action that could or should be taken. The PFD procedure would be thwarted if coroners, who are entrusted by Parliament to take sensitive and difficult decisions, did not regard the procedure as being a realistic one.

72. We would endorse the Chief Coroner's Guidance, para 4, which states that PFD reports should (among other things) be meaningful and, wherever possible, designed to have practical effect. On this basis, it is open to a coroner to take into consideration whether there is any realistic prospect, including on resource grounds, that a PFD report will be acted upon by its recipient. In any event, resource considerations were not in this case central to the Coroner's decision."

CHAPTER FIFTEEN

CHALLENGING DECISIONS OF THE CORONER AND FRESH INQUESTS

There are two routes to challenge any aspect of the inquest or to appeal for a fresh inquest:

1. Judicial Review;

2. A statutory application for a fresh inquest under section 13 of the Coroners Act 1988 (section 13 is still in force).

JUDICIAL REVIEW

Judicial Review is not an appeal as such; rather, it is a review of a decision-making process. Accordingly, a person cannot judicially review the decision of the coroner or the conclusion of the inquest simply because they do not like it: one of the high thresholds for Judicial Review must be met.

Judicial review is in itself a rather complex topic with a strong body of caselaw. Should you be intending to bring a challenge by way of judicial review then it would be wise to consult a specialist textbook on the subject. The below is, however, intended to give a broad outline of the key principles with which you should be acquainted.

GROUNDS OF REVIEW

There are three common grounds of review:

1. The decision made was illegal;

2. The decision made was unreasonable or irrational;

3. There was procedural impropriety or unfairness.

In relation to the first ground, 'illegality' means the decision being challenged did not fall within the boundaries of law. An example might be that the coroner acted outside the bounds of their powers. Another may be that they misapplied the relevant legislation.

In relation to the second ground, 'unreasonable' (which tends to be interchangeable with 'irrational') is often described as needing to meet the standard of 'Wednesbury unreasonable'. That is a standard drawn from the case of *Associated Provincial Picture Houses Ltd v Wednesbury Corporation* (1984) 1 KB 223. For a decision to satisfy this threshold, it must be so unreasonable that no reasonable person acting reasonably could have made it. It is, therefore, a high hurdle to cross.

Finally, the third ground of 'procedural impropriety' or 'unfairness' can include scenarios such as where there is bias, or where a person who had a right to be heard (or consulted) was not.

PROCEDURE

Step 1: Pre-action protocol

A person contemplating bringing judicial review proceedings should comply with the pre-action protocol for judicial review and send a letter before claim to the proposed defendant. They must then allow time for a response letter before the claim form is issued.

Step 2: issuing a claim form

The claim form must then be issued on Form N461 (available on the government website). That form must set out the essentials of the claim but must also state: a) whether there are likely to be any interested parties; b) that the claimant is seeking permission to proceed with a claim for judicial review; and c) what remedy, including any interim relief, the claimant is seeking[31]. The claim form must also be accompanied by a number of other documents including a statement of the grounds for bringing the application for judicial review, a statement of the facts relied upon and any written evidence that the claimant seeks to rely upon[32].

By virtue of Rule 54.5(1) of the Civil Procedure Rules ("CPR"), the claim form must be filed: a) promptly; and b) in any event no later than three months after the grounds to make the claim first arose.

Rule 54.5(2) of the CPR provides that the time limits in this rule may not be extended by agreement between the parties.

The Court does have the power to extend time under Rule 3.1(2)(a) of the CPR but will only do so where 'good reason' is shown.

If the matter is urgent, it is possible to apply for an expedited hearing, using form N463.

Step 3: Defendant's summary grounds

Any person who is served with the claim form and wishes to take part in the judicial review must file and serve an acknowledgment of service. This is served on form N462, along with summary grounds of defence[33].

If that person does not serve an acknowledgment of service, they will be barred from taking part in any hearing to determine whether permission should be given (but not otherwise barred from taking part in a hearing if permission is granted)[34].

---

[31] See Rule 54.6 of the CPR

[32] See CPR Practice Direction 54A, paragraph 5.6

[33] Rule 54.8 of the CPR

[34] Rule 54.9(1) of the CPR

Permission

The papers are then put before a High Court judge, who determines whether permission to proceed with judicial review should be granted.

The test applied by the Judge is arguability – i.e. "*on a quick perusal of the material then available, the court thinks that it discloses what might on further consideration turn out to be an arguable case*"[35].

If the Judge grants permission, then directions are laid down for the substantive hearing[36]. If permission is not granted, then the claimant does have the right to renew their application orally unless the Judge has certified it as being 'totally without merit' on the papers[37].

The substantive hearing

At the hearing, if either party wishes to rely on oral evidence, including cross-examination of witnesses, that party must apply for a direction to that effect[38].

REMEDIES

There are a number of remedies available following a successful judicial review. These include, most commonly:

- A mandatory order – this is an order mandating the defendant to take some particular action. An example in this context may be that the Court orders a fresh inquest;

---

35 *R(National Federation of Self-Employed and Small Business Ltd) v Inland Revenue Commissioners* (1982) AC 617 at 644A

36 Rule 54.14 of the CPR

37 Rule 54.12 of the CPR

38 *Bubb v Wandsworth LBC* (2011) EWCA Civ 1285

- A prohibiting order – this is an order prohibiting the defendant from taking a certain action, such as disclosure;

- A quashing order – this is an order quashing the decision of the defendant. It may well be coupled with a mandatory order. For example, the conclusion reached by the coroner may be quashed with a mandatory order to conduct a fresh inquest.

- Issue a declaration – this is a declaration of the position in law.

The claim form will require the claimant to identify the remedy sought.

APPEALING A JUDICIAL REVIEW DECISION

Appeals to unsuccessful applications for judicial review are heard by the Court of Appeal.

RELEVANT CASES

<u>R v HM Coroner for Inner London West District ex p. Dallaglio (1994) 4 All ER 139</u>

This was a case where the Court of Appeal considered the question of possible bias on the part of the coroner.

The inquests, after the Marchioness disaster, were adjourned pending the outcome of criminal proceedings. The coroner was reported as describing some of the relatives of the deceased as 'unhinged' and 'mentally unwell'.

Once the criminal proceedings were concluded, the coroner sought the views of the deceased's families as to the resumption of the inquests. He refused to remove himself from conducting the inquest on the grounds of apparent bias. He also refused to resume the inquests. The families challenged his decisions by way of judicial review. That application having been refused, the case made its way to the Court of Appeal.

The higher Court allowed the appeal. In so doing it held that the applicants only had to show that there was a real danger that bias had affected the decision, albeit unconsciously. On the facts of this case, the use of the expressions 'unhinged' and 'mentally unwell' did indicate a real possibility of unconscious bias. Accordingly, the coroner's decision was quashed and the matter was remitted to a different coroner for a fresh decision on whether to resume the inquests.

R (Makki) v HM Senior Coroner for South Manchester (2023) EWHC 80 (Admin)

The claimant was the father of the deceased, Yousef Makki, who died at the age of 17 as a result of a single stab wound to his chest. The interested party, a boy called Joshua Molnar, accepted that he wielded the flick knife which caused the fatal injury. He had been tried for murder in 2019 and was acquitted, after successfully claiming that he was acting in self-defence.

The inquest – which had been suspended pending the criminal proceedings – was resumed between 8 and 17 November 2021. The coroner concluded that there was insufficient evidence to determine whether the killing was lawful or unlawful. She therefore returned a narrative conclusion, in which she said "*The precise circumstances in which he was wounded cannot, on the balance of probabilities, be ascertained.*"

The claimant applied to judicially review the coroner's decision that there was insufficient evidence on whether the killing was unlawful, on the grounds that it was *Wednesbury* unreasonable because – he said – the coroner failed to properly consider all the evidence in reaching that conclusion.

In granting the application for Judicial Review, the Court made the following comments on the adequacy of the coroner's consideration of the evidence:

> "*42. I do not discern any attempt to analyse the "precise sequence of events" immediately leading to the fatal stabbing. There is no*

indication that HMSC assessed the reliability of JM's evidence to the inquest. (I do not accept Mr Webster's submission that she must obviously have rejected it, for otherwise she would have found self-defence, since it is not possible to discern what consideration she gave to the two elements of self-defence and which evidence she regarded to be relevant and reliable.) HMSC noted that JM lied immediately after the stabbing "to mislead attention away from himself," but seemingly disregards this factor because it was dealt with in "another jurisdiction." She recounts his evidence, including that he was "feeling hard done by" and was angry and provoked by YM's name calling immediately prior to drawing his knife, but she does not indicate what conclusions, if any, she draws from his evidence.

44. Consequently, whilst I do not consider that the evidence necessarily all points in one direction, neither can I be satisfied that HMSC has assessed all relevant evidence or analysed the findings of fact she made. HMSC's generic reference to her consideration of the "totality" of the evidence is inadequate to convey that she did 'strive' to reach a conclusion upon the evidence. If she did so but was left profoundly unsure then she did not explain why."

STATUTORY APPLICATION FOR A FRESH INQUEST

GROUNDS OF APPLICATION

Section 13 of the Coroners Act 1988 states as follows:

"***13.— Order to hold investigation.***

(1) This section applies where, on an application by or under the authority of the Attorney-General, the High Court is satisfied as respects a coroner ("the coroner concerned") either—

> *(a) that he refuses or neglects to hold an inquest or an investigation which ought to be held; or*

> *(b) where an inquest or an investigation has been held by him, that (whether by reason of fraud, rejection of evidence, irregularity of proceedings, insufficiency of inquiry, the discovery of new facts or evidence or otherwise) it is necessary or desirable in the interests of justice that an investigation (or as the case may by, another investigation) should be held.*
>
> *(2) The High Court may—*
>
> *(a) order an investigation under Part 1 of the Coroners and Justice Act 2009 to be held into the death either—*
>
> *(i) by the coroner concerned; or*
>
> *(ii) by [a senior coroner, area coroner or assistant coroner in the same coroner area;*
>
> *(b) order the coroner concerned to pay such costs of and incidental to the application as to the court may appear just; and*
>
> *(c) where an inquest has been held, quash any inquisition on, or determination or finding made at that inquest."*

The statute requires that the application is made either by, or under the authority of, the Attorney-General. It follows that any person who wishes to ask for an inquest / a fresh inquest under this provision must first petition the Attorney-General.

That is done by asking the Attorney-General for a *fiat* – i.e. a process by which the Attorney-General grants his or her consent to enable persons to commence legal proceedings in his or her name. The grounds on which the *fiat* can be sought are as set out in the statute – i.e. the coroner has not held an inquest which they ought to have done, or the inquest has taken place but is deficient for some reason. Once the *fiat* is granted then the application can be made.

PROCEDURE

Any person who is dissatisfied with the lack of inquest or, where an inquest has been held, with that inquest by reason of some irregularity or (more often) because of new facts and evidence having come to light can apply to the Senior Law Office to consider whether to refer the matter to the High Court.

There is no specific procedure for applying to the Attorney-General and a letter setting out the grounds may suffice.

If the Attorney-General does give his or her authority to the person petitioning for a new inquest, the latter can then make an application to the High Court under section 13 of the Coroners Act 1988.

RELEVANT CASES

<u>Attorney-General v HM Coroner for South Yorkshire (West) (2012) EWHC 3783</u>

This was an application on behalf of the relatives of 96 Liverpool football fans who died at Hillsborough Stadium in 1989, in an infamously tragic case of mass asphyxiation.

At the inquest the jury was informed that it was an inquiry only into the identity of V and when and where V had died. The coroner decided to impose a 3.15 pm cut-off on the inquiry which meant that only the events leading up to that point on the day, when the first ambulance arrived on the pitch, were included in the inquest. The jury returned a verdict of accidental death. The families of V found the inquest wholly inadequate but repeated attempts to overturn the verdict had failed. In 2009, an independent panel was set up to investigate the events that led to V's deaths. The instant application was made under the Coroners Act 1988 s.13 as a result of the panel's findings published in September 2012. The issue was whether the interests of justice made a further inquest desirable or necessary.

The application was granted.

The Court held that the report produced for the application cast new light on the circumstances in which the deceased met their death. Perhaps the most dramatic and distressing was the fact that after the 3:15p.m. cut off point imposed by the coroner in the first inquest there was evidence that in some cases death might have been reversible; so the events after that time were relevant to the cause of death. There were, though, a number of other considerations which reinforced the conclusion that the original inquest should be quashed.

In quashing the original inquest decision, then, and ordering a fresh inquest the Court held:

> "*29. This combination of circumstances, as we have narrated, makes inevitable the order for a new inquest. The interests of justice must be served. Within the limits of the coronial system, the facts must be investigated and reanalysed in a fresh inquest when, however distressing or unpalatable, the truth will be brought to light. In this way the families of those who died in this disaster will be vindicated and the memory of each victim will be properly respected.*
>
> *30. All the inquisitions will be quashed. There will be new inquests in each and every case. The legislation relating to venue is, as we have said in argument, problematic. The inquests will be remitted to another coroner for the same administrative area as the original inquests: in relation to the 95 victims the South Yorkshire (East) area at Doncaster; and in relation to the inquest into Anthony Bland, to the West Yorkshire (West) Coroner at Bradford.*"

<u>Bell v HM Coroner for South Yorkshire (2023) 3 WLUK 342</u>

The applicant was the brother of the deceased, a woman who was killed when she walked into the path of an oncoming train. She had a long history of serious mental health problems. She had also, whilst a patient in a hospital for her mental health, undertaken some work as a ward aid during which time she began a relationship with a student nurse. That relationship resulted in a pregnancy and termination; the relationship then ended and she moved to live with her mother with whom she had a difficult relationship.

The inquest into her death, held in 1992, recorded an open verdict. In 1999 the hospital at which she had been a patient closed, following an investigation and report which concluded that there had been a systematic failure to prevent a culture of unprofessional and degrading practices towards patients.

In 1999 the deceased's mother told the applicant about the deceased's sexual relationship with the student nurse, her pregnancy and termination. The applicant subsequently reported that relationship to the police as an offence under section 128 of the Mental Health Act 1959. Initially the police considered there to be insufficient evidence to proceed with the matter; in 2016 the police reviewed that decision and the Crown Prosecution Service found that there was sufficient evidence of an offence, but the nurse's prosecution was not in the public interest. In 2017, the applicant asked the coroner to conduct a new inquest on the basis of fresh evidence as to the deceased's state of mind at the time of her death – namely, the inappropriate relationship and the inadequate way in which the hospital had treated her. The coroner declined to conduct a new inquest and the applicant accordingly applied in 2022 to the High Court under section 13 of the Coroners Act 1988.

The application was refused.

In refusing the application, the High Court held *per* William Davis LJ that the only basis on which a fresh inquest could be ordered under section 13(1)(b) of the Coroners Act 1988 was the discovery of new facts or evidence. That did not mean 'any' evidence; there had to be cogent evidence. The Court held, therefore, that while it had sympathy with the claimant, it was not satisfied that the statutory criteria were met.

ANNEX

RECORD OF INQUEST

Form 2
Record of an inquest

The following is the record of the inquest (including the statutory determination and, where required, findings)—

1. Name of the deceased (if known):

2. Medical cause of death:

3. How, when and where, and for investigations where section 5(2) of the Coroners and Justice Act 2009 applies, in what circumstances the deceased came by his or her death: (see note (ii)):

4. Conclusion of the coroner/ jury as to the death: (see notes (i) and (ii):

5. Further particulars required by the Births and Deaths Registration Act 1953 to be registered concerning the death:

1.	2.	3.	4.	5.	6.
Date and place of death	Name and surname of deceased	Sex	Maiden surname of woman who has married	Date and place of birth	Occupation and usual address

Signature of coroner (and jurors):

NOTES:

(i) One of the following short-form conclusions may be adopted:—

I. accident or misadventure

II. alcohol / drug related

III. industrial disease

IV. lawful/ unlawful killing

V. natural causes

VI. open

VII. road traffic collision

VIII. stillbirth

IX. suicide

(ii) As an alternative, or in addition to one of the short-form conclusions listed under NOTE (i), the coroner or where applicable the jury, may make a brief narrative conclusion.

(iii) The standard of proof required for the short form conclusions of "unlawful killing" and "suicide" is the criminal standard of proof. For all other short-form conclusions and a narrative statement the standard of proof is the civil standard of proof.

MORE BOOKS BY
LAW BRIEF PUBLISHING

A selection of our other titles available now:-

'A Practical Guide to Estate Administration and Crypto Assets' by Richard Marshall
'A Practical Guide to Managing GDPR Data Subject Access Requests – Second Edition' by Patrick O'Kane
'A Practical Guide to Parental Alienation in Private and Public Law Children Cases' by Sam King QC & Frankie Shama
'Contested Heritage – Removing Art from Land and Historic Buildings' by Richard Harwood QC, Catherine Dobson, David Sawtell
'The Limits of Separate Legal Personality: When Those Running a Company Can Be Held Personally Liable for Losses Caused to Third Parties Outside of the Company' by Dr Mike Wilkinson
'A Practical Guide to Transgender Law' by Robin Moira White & Nicola Newbegin
'A Practical Guide to 'Stranded Spouses' in Family Law' by Mani Singh Basi
'A Practical Guide to Residential Freehold Conveyancing' by Lorraine Richardson
'A Practical Guide to Pensions on Divorce for Lawyers' by Bryan Scant
'A Practical Guide to Challenging Sham Marriage Allegations in Immigration Law' by Priya Solanki
'A Practical Guide to Legal Rights in Scotland' by Sarah-Jane Macdonald
'A Practical Guide to New Build Conveyancing' by Paul Sams & Rebecca East
'A Practical Guide to Defending Barristers in Disciplinary Cases' by Marc Beaumont
'A Practical Guide to Inherited Wealth on Divorce' by Hayley Trim
'A Practical Guide to Practice Direction 12J and Domestic Abuse in Private Law Children Proceedings' by Rebecca Cross & Malvika Jaganmohan
'A Practical Guide to Confiscation and Restraint' by Narita Bahra QC, John Carl Townsend, David Winch
'A Practical Guide to the Law of Forests in Scotland' by Philip Buchan
'A Practical Guide to Health and Medical Cases in Immigration Law' by Rebecca Chapman & Miranda Butler

‘A Practical Guide to Bad Character Evidence for Criminal Practitioners by Aparna Rao
‘A Practical Guide to Extradition Law post-Brexit’ by Myles Grandison et al
‘A Practical Guide to Hoarding and Mental Health for Housing Lawyers’ by Rachel Coyle
‘A Practical Guide to Psychiatric Claims in Personal Injury – 2nd Edition’ by Liam Ryan
‘Stephens on Contractual Indemnities’ by Richard Stephens
‘A Practical Guide to the EU Succession Regulation’ by Richard Frimston
‘A Practical Guide to Solicitor and Client Costs – 2nd Edition’ by Robin Dunne
‘Constructive Dismissal – Practice Pointers and Principles’ by Benjimin Burgher
‘A Practical Guide to Religion and Belief Discrimination Claims in the Workplace’ by Kashif Ali
‘A Practical Guide to the Law of Medical Treatment Decisions’ by Ben Troke
‘Fundamental Dishonesty and QOCS in Personal Injury Proceedings: Law and Practice’ by Jake Rowley
‘A Practical Guide to the Law in Relation to School Exclusions’ by Charlotte Hadfield & Alice de Coverley
‘A Practical Guide to Divorce for the Silver Separators’ by Karin Walker
‘The Right to be Forgotten – The Law and Practical Issues’ by Melissa Stock
‘A Practical Guide to Planning Law and Rights of Way in National Parks, the Broads and AONBs’ by James Maurici QC, James Neill et al
‘A Practical Guide to Election Law’ by Tom Tabori
‘A Practical Guide to the Law in Relation to Surrogacy’ by Andrew Powell
‘A Practical Guide to Claims Arising from Fatal Accidents – 2nd Edition’ by James Patience
‘A Practical Guide to the Ownership of Employee Inventions – From Entitlement to Compensation’ by James Tumbridge & Ashley Roughton
‘A Practical Guide to Asbestos Claims’ by Jonathan Owen & Gareth McAloon
‘A Practical Guide to Stamp Duty Land Tax in England and Northern Ireland’ by Suzanne O’Hara
‘A Practical Guide to the Law of Farming Partnerships’ by Philip Whitcomb
‘Covid-19, Homeworking and the Law – The Essential Guide to Employment and GDPR Issues’ by Forbes Solicitors
‘Covid-19 and Criminal Law – The Essential Guide’ by Ramya Nagesh

'Covid-19 and Family Law in England and Wales – The Essential Guide' by Safda Mahmood
'A Practical Guide to the Law of Unlawful Eviction and Harassment – 2nd Edition' by Stephanie Lovegrove
'Covid-19, Brexit and the Law of Commercial Leases – The Essential Guide' by Mark Shelton
'A Practical Guide to Costs in Personal Injury Claims – 2nd Edition' by Matthew Hoe
'A Practical Guide to the General Data Protection Regulation (GDPR) – 2nd Edition' by Keith Markham
'Ellis on Credit Hire – Sixth Edition' by Aidan Ellis & Tim Kevan
'A Practical Guide to Working with Litigants in Person and McKenzie Friends in Family Cases' by Stuart Barlow
'Protecting Unregistered Brands: A Practical Guide to the Law of Passing Off' by Lorna Brazell
'A Practical Guide to Secondary Liability and Joint Enterprise Post-Jogee' by Joanne Cecil & James Mehigan
'A Practical Guide to the Pre-Action RTA Claims Protocol for Personal Injury Lawyers' by Antonia Ford
'A Practical Guide to Neighbour Disputes and the Law' by Alexander Walsh
'A Practical Guide to Forfeiture of Leases' by Mark Shelton
'A Practical Guide to Coercive Control for Legal Practitioners and Victims' by Rachel Horman
'Tackling Disclosure in the Criminal Courts – A Practitioner's Guide' by Narita Bahra QC & Don Ramble
'A Practical Guide to the Law of Driverless Cars – Second Edition' by Alex Glassbrook, Emma Northey & Scarlett Milligan
'A Practical Guide to TOLATA Claims' by Greg Williams
'A Practical Guide to Elderly Law – 2nd Edition' by Justin Patten
'A Practical Guide to Responding to Housing Disrepair and Unfitness Claims' by Iain Wightwick
'A Practical Guide to the Law of Bullying and Harassment in the Workplace' by Philip Hyland
'How to Be a Freelance Solicitor: A Practical Guide to the SRA-Regulated Freelance Solicitor Model' by Paul Bennett
'A Practical Guide to Prison Injury Claims' by Malcolm Johnson

'A Practical Guide to the Small Claims Track – 2nd Edition' by Dominic Bright
'A Practical Guide to Advising Clients at the Police Station' by Colin Stephen McKeown-Beaumont
'A Practical Guide to Antisocial Behaviour Injunctions' by Iain Wightwick
'Practical Mediation: A Guide for Mediators, Advocates, Advisers, Lawyers, and Students in Civil, Commercial, Business, Property, Workplace, and Employment Cases' by Jonathan Dingle with John Sephton
'The Mini-Pupillage Workbook' by David Boyle
'A Practical Guide to Crofting Law' by Brian Inkster
'A Practical Guide to the Law of Domain Names and Cybersquatting' by Andrew Clemson
'A Practical Guide to the Law of Gender Pay Gap Reporting' by Harini Iyengar
'NHS Whistleblowing and the Law' by Joseph England
'Employment Law and the Gig Economy' by Nigel Mackay & Annie Powell
'A Practical Guide to Noise Induced Hearing Loss (NIHL) Claims' by Andrew Mckie, Ian Skeate, Gareth McAloon
'An Introduction to Beauty Negligence Claims – A Practical Guide for the Personal Injury Practitioner' by Greg Almond
'Intercompany Agreements for Transfer Pricing Compliance' by Paul Sutton
'Zen and the Art of Mediation' by Martin Plowman
'A Practical Guide to the SRA Principles, Individual and Law Firm Codes of Conduct 2019 – What Every Law Firm Needs to Know' by Paul Bennett
'A Practical Guide to Adoption for Family Lawyers' by Graham Pegg
'A Practical Guide to Industrial Disease Claims' by Andrew Mckie & Ian Skeate
'A Practical Guide to Redundancy' by Philip Hyland
'A Practical Guide to Vicarious Liability' by Mariel Irvine
'A Practical Guide to Applications for Landlord's Consent and Variation of Leases' by Mark Shelton
'A Practical Guide to Relief from Sanctions Post-Mitchell and Denton' by Peter Causton
'A Practical Guide to Equity Release for Advisors' by Paul Sams
'A Practical Guide to Financial Services Claims' by Chris Hegarty
'The Law of Houses in Multiple Occupation: A Practical Guide to HMO Proceedings' by Julian Hunt

‘Occupiers, Highways and Defective Premises Claims: A Practical Guide Post-Jackson – 2nd Edition’ by Andrew Mckie
‘A Practical Guide to Financial Ombudsman Service Claims’ by Adam Temple & Robert Scrivenor
‘A Practical Guide to Running Housing Disrepair and Cavity Wall Claims: 2nd Edition’ by Andrew Mckie & Ian Skeate
‘A Practical Guide to Holiday Sickness Claims – 2nd Edition’ by Andrew Mckie & Ian Skeate
‘Arguments and Tactics for Personal Injury and Clinical Negligence Claims’ by Dorian Williams
‘A Practical Guide to Drone Law’ by Rufus Ballaster, Andrew Firman, Eleanor Clot
‘A Practical Guide to Compliance for Personal Injury Firms Working With Claims Management Companies’ by Paul Bennett
‘RTA Allegations of Fraud in a Post-Jackson Era: The Handbook – 2nd Edition’ by Andrew Mckie
‘RTA Personal Injury Claims: A Practical Guide Post-Jackson’ by Andrew Mckie
‘On Experts: CPR35 for Lawyers and Experts’ by David Boyle
‘An Introduction to Personal Injury Law’ by David Boyle

www.ingramcontent.com/pod-product-compliance
Lightning Source LLC
LaVergne TN
LVHW052309200926
848481LV00002B/512